MW00441934

WHEN THE BOTTOM FALLS OUT

Redemption's Greatest Story NEVER Told

WHEN THE BOTTOM FALLS OUT

Redemption's Greatest Story **NEVER** Told

JIM GOODROE

When the Bottom Falls Out: Redemption's Greatest Story NEVER Told

© 2023 Jim Goodroe

All Rights Reserved

Cover art: "Mouth of the Earth," by artist Yoram Ranaan. Used by permission.

Unless otherwise noted, all Scripture quotations are from the ESV® Bible (The Holy Bible, English Standard Version®), copyright © 2001 by Crossway Bibles, a publishing ministry of Good News Publishers. Used by permission. All rights reserved.

Scripture quotations marked KJV are taken from the Holy Bible, King James Version. Public domain.

Scripture quotations taken from the (NASB®) New American Standard Bible®, Copyright © 1960, 1971, 1977, 1995, 2020 by The Lockman Foundation. Used by permission. All rights reserved. www.lockman.org.

Scripture quotations marked (NIV) are taken from the Holy Bible, New International Version®, NIV®. Copyright © 1973, 1978, 1984, 2011 by Biblica, Inc.™ Used by permission of Zondervan. All rights reserved worldwide. www.zondervan.com The "NIV" and "New International Version" are trademarks registered in the United States Patent and Trademark Office by Biblica, Inc.™

Scripture taken from the New King James Version®. Copyright © 1982 by Thomas Nelson. Used by permission. All rights reserved.

Scripture quotations marked (NLT) are taken from the Holy Bible, New Living Translation, copyright ©1996, 2004, 2015 by Tyndale House Foundation. Used by permission of Tyndale House Publishers, Carol Stream, Illinois 60188. All rights reserved.

ISBN 978-1-955295-37-6

Courier Publishing
100 Manly Street
Greenvile, South Carolina 29601
CourierPublishing.com

PUBLISHED IN THE UNITED STATES OF AMERICA

DEDICATION

This book is dedicated to Dr. Jerry Vines, one of America's premier preachers and Bible expositors for decades on both sides of Y2K. He ordained me twice: as the youngest deacon ever elected in the churches he pastored, then two years later as a pastor myself. I caught his love for God's Word, hearing him preach Sunday mornings and evenings for two years, from my perch in the choir loft behind him. I caught his love for lost souls, when for weeks he took me with him on evangelistic visitation, where I learned how to use the Romans Road* to lead people to Christ.

Years later, one cold night between Christmas and New Year's, I had the opportunity to attend his annual "all night" reunion. He poured his deep wisdom and practical pointers into the dozens of "preacher boys" who answered the call under his ministry. We idolized him, but that night he bared his soul as he shared how "the bottom fell out" at the mega-church he had left our church to pastor. His outline was a story line from an Old Testament book, but his outtakes were scars from the painful attacks on his pastoral leadership there. If the bottom could fall out on such a choice servant as Brother Jerry, then nobody was exempt!

This bruising Bible story of "Korah's rebellion" stuck with me through decades of study, meditation, and even imagination. I saw the varied ways the bottom fell out on the other major actors and minor players in the story, as it does on each of us. Most blew out, but others bounced back! "Now these things happened to them as an example, but they were written down for our instruction, on whom the end of the ages has come" (1 Corinthians 10:11).

When and however the bottom falls out on you, profit from these principles and the Lord's presence as you battle back to put your life back together.

* See Appendices in back of this book for the Romans Road gospel presentation. If you know Jesus, you may use this to share the gospel with others. What if you have not yet entered into a personal relationship with Christ, or are not sure you would go to Heaven if you died tonight?

Walk down the Romans Road for yourself, following the instructions there.

INTRODUCTION

We all face times when "the bottom falls out." Sometimes it comes at the worst times. As I was writing this page the day after New Year's, I received a text from a close friend that read, "My brother's wife died suddenly on Tuesday morning after Christmas."

The bottom fell out on my parents the day after my twin sister and I were born. My sister died — and just two days after the joy of our family having doubled in size, my father faced the grim task of buying a family cemetery plot. To live on earth means our story line will be invaded by times when the bottom falls out. I've had a cemetery plot my whole life.

I was almost seven the first time that I remember the bottom falling out. My early life had been great in a small southern town. It was the "Baby Boom," so our neighborhood had lots of boys my age. We spent our free time outdoors, having a great time. I was made for school and had loved kindergarten and first grade. But this two-year bliss came to a screeching halt. We vacated the only house I'd ever known and left the town where all our relatives lived. We moved hours away where nobody knew us. I encountered gnats gnawing my neck and short-sleeved arms and sand spurs barbing my bare feet.

The good news is that we did not stay here long. The bad news was that a bad business venture bankrupted us. The bottom fell out seven more times over the next five years. Dad kept chasing better jobs, and I kept changing schools, eight times. In this revolving door, we left any friends I'd made. Five times we changed cities and churches, and twice we changed states.

God's providence put this on hold my third-grade year. I finished second-grade and got halfway through fourth grade in the best house ever with a vacant lot next door, where we played ball. The lot lay across the street from a church I came to love, where I learned how much God loved me and how He proved His love. God left me in one place long enough to meet Jesus for myself. Wherever we moved, we joined a church just like the one we had left, so church and family were my stability in a world of shifting sands. Jesus became my refuge and strength, and our relationship has grown for two-thirds of a century.

Years of sudden change prepared me for a teenage trauma when again the bottom fell out. These constant moves taught me to go with the flow, make the best of it, and initiate conversations with strangers. Loving parents had always provided everything I needed. We rarely ate out, so I never even had to decide what to eat, much less how to procure and prepare it.

During the second week of my sixteen-year-old summer, I was at the beach on a church youth retreat. The first long-distance call I ever received brought the news that our senator had offered me a job in Washington for the rest of the summer. It sounded like the opportunity of a lifetime, so I quickly said yes. Days later, my parents took me to Atlanta for my overnight train ride to D.C. At sunrise, I stepped off with my suitcase at Union Station and walked to the Capitol buildings I could see in the distance.

Shuffled from one office to another, I discovered I was too young for the promised job. The good news is that there was one job I was old enough for: Page in the Senate. The bad news? It included no super-vision, transportation, or lodging once my weekday workday ended. I spent the summer as an unaccompanied minor in the largest city I'd ever seen. The good news? This experience would show me that "God is

… a very present help in trouble … though the earth gives way" (Psalm 46:1-2). When the bottom falls out, look to the top.

You, too, may feel hopeless from your fallout. You may see no help on the horizon. There may be no way you can envision your life turning around or anything you could see making a difference. But don't give up hope. There's a plot twist in our Bible story. A happy ending is tucked away in a later, obscure passage most readers have overlooked. You will find it as this book unfolds. It is redemption's greatest story never told. Its buried treasure can change your story when the bottom falls out on you.

CONTENTS

Part One

Victims: The Saga of the Sons of Korah

Chapter 1 ....Who's Who... 3

Chapter 2 ....Showdown at Sunset: Korah, Moses, and Aaron......... 9

Chapter 3 ....Mr. Identity Crisis: Moses 25

Chapter 4 ....Bad Blood: Korah 39

Chapter 5 ....Aaron, Also 53

Chapter 6 ....Reuben, Reuben: Dathan and Abiram...................... 63

Chapter 7 ....Aaron, Solo... 77

Chapter 8 ....Flashback 85

Chapter 9 ....The Night Before the Morning After 105

Chapter 10 ....Show Up for Showdown 115

Chapter 11 ....New Thing/Old Hat: Moses 125

Chapter 12 ....Something New: Korah, Dathan, and Abiram 131

Chapter 13 ....Censured: Korah's 250 Chiefs 137

Chapter 14 ....Victimized: Sons of Korah 143

Chapter 15 ....Joint Chiefs? 153

Chapter 16 ....From Victims to Victors: Sons of Korah 159

Part Two

Victors: The Songs of the Sons of Korah

(in likely chronological order)

Psalm 88.. 167

Psalm 84.. 173

Psalm 46.. 177

Psalm 42..181

Psalm 43..185

Psalm 44..189

Psalm 85..193

Psalm 45..197

Psalm 47..201

Psalm 48..205

Psalm 49..209

Psalm 87..213

Appendices

Acknowledgments...217

The Romans Road 221

The Jewish Historical Writings 223

Why Study the Old Testament? 227

How the Levites Were Special...................................231

WHEN THE BOTTOM FALLS OUT

Redemption's Greatest Story **NEVER** Told

VICTIMS: THE SAGA OF THE SONS OF KORAH

CHAPTER 1

WHO'S WHO

For I have come to set a man against his father … . Whoever loves father or mother more than me is not worthy of me … . Whoever finds his life will lose it, and whoever loses his life for my sake will find it (Matthew 10:35, 37, 39).

God is our refuge and strength, a very present help in trouble. Therefore we will not fear though the earth gives way (Psalm 46:1–2a).

Long ago and far away, teenage brothers I have nicknamed Ace, Elk, and Abe penned the above words in Psalm 46. They watched the earth give way, literally. A sudden sinkhole swallowed their family tent with their parents in it. As they stood by in wide-eyed shock, the earth's surface around the hole closed itself, like a monster's mouth after eating a meal. The Bible knows these boys and their descendants as "the sons of Korah." This book is the rest of their story and how it shows how God is our refuge and our strength.

This Bible story has one implosion whose results are strewn through its pages, a shred here, a bit of evidence there. Pieced together, they tell redemption's greatest story *never* told. The Scriptures themselves provide most of its facts, far more than just a skeletal outline. My account is a historical Bible story. To bring the story to life, I have fleshed out what seems like a likely scenario by deducing and developing what the Bible does not say. Where the Bible leaves out details, I acknowledge this, sometimes suggesting a likely scenario.

The Lord sowed several seeds in my spiritual psyche, which converged to propel my fascination and investigation of this story. Research within our Bible, plus Jewish historical writings, sewed enough pieces together that little patchwork was needed.

Because God guarantees His Word, He is very protective of it. Proverbs 30:5–6 cautions, "Every word of God proves true … . Do not add to his words, lest he rebuke you and you be found a liar." Four verses from the end of the Bible, Revelation 22:18 echoes, "I warn everyone who hears the words of the prophecy of this book: if anyone adds to them, God will add to him the plagues described in this book." When Bible events are fleshed out, the storyteller walks a fine line. As you read these chapters, source Scriptures are referenced, and printed verbatim within the chapter. Plausible detail or dialogue in the scriptural events or action is added within the text of the chapter. Where actions or events are projected into the story, to fill in the gaps, they are prefaced with a disclaimer such as, "It may have happened this way." Where others have suggested such details, outside sources are acknowledged.

Two Bible reading patterns converged as my treasure hunt clues to this thriller. After many readings, Korah's rebellion and its horrific judgment began to act itself out in my mind like a movie. My daily devotional default plan has tried to cover Psalms and Proverbs every month, by reading the Proverbs chapter number matching the date of the month, plus five Psalms. On most months, my reading included Psalms 42–49 and 84–88, where twelve psalms are attributed to the sons of Korah. This seems contradictory, as the primary account of Korah's rebellion in Numbers 16:20–35 (especially verses 27 and 32) implies that the earth swallowed Korah's **entire** family.

Evangelicals at large hold this misconception. A well-known Bible teacher put it this way in 1997: "The Lord opened up the earth and it swallowed Korah, Dathan, and Abiram *and their entire families*" (emphasis mine). The buried treasure I stumbled on to solve the mystery is Numbers' later recap of its earlier fifty-verse story with a three-verse summary (26:9–11). The clincher is verse 11, which has eluded the attention of most Bible readers: "But the sons of Korah did not die."

Had Korah's sons been swallowed by the earth with their father, the Bible and its story would be missing more than just them and their twelve psalms. It would be missing one of the Old Testament's top five characters, Samuel, and the two books he wrote. Samuel's great-grand-father to the thirteenth generation was Abiasaph (Ebiasaph), Korah's third son (1 Chronicles 6:33–38). Thirteen was not unlucky back then but consider how unfortunate would have been the loss of Samuel.

Samuel was Israel's last judge and first prophet. The high priestly line jumped from Eli's branch in Levi's family tree to Samuel's line. He anointed Israel's first two kings, Saul and David. He wrote First and Second Samuel and included spiritual gems not mined elsewhere, which surfaced from the events they recorded. About the first king he anointed, he wrote, "To obey is better than sacrifice … for rebellion is as the sin of witchcraft" (1 Samuel 15:22–23, NKJV). About the second king he anointed, he wrote, "Man looks on the outward appearance, but the LORD looks on the heart" (1 Samuel 16:7).

Curiosity may send readers to Numbers 26:9–11 to verify these survivors of Korah's rebellion and Numbers 16 for the Bible story. To check out the Psalms of the sons of Korah, we can start with 46:1–2 and 84:10–12. These passages will jump off the page and come alive, once you know what Paul Harvey called "the rest of the story." Read God's book any way you want. But I suggest you read my book like a novel.

Part One is the story line, "Victims: The Saga of the Sons of Korah."

It opens at the showdown between Korah's crew and Moses, as God's representatives and rebels wait with bated breath to see whether and how the Lord will settle this dispute. Then we flash back the main characters, as ironic details develop what brought them to the showdown (the hinge point in the story). Numbers' second chapter after the showdown suggests the next events in the lives of the sons of Korah.

Each of the main characters in the story had the bottom fall out. Like life, these dives dart at various times in diverse ways, with different stakes and drastic outcomes. Some are final, even fatal. Others are remedial. "The righteous falls seven times and rises again, but the wicked stumble in times of calamity" (Proverbs 24:16). Don't give up, get up! When the bottom falls out on you, battle back.

Part One, "The Saga," is the bulk of the book. This in-depth Bible study details how the bottom fell out on the major players and minor people in this true story. To better relate their ancient actions to our times and to personalize them for you, treat these chunks of text like backstory. Speed-read them the first time. Flow with the mainstream to develop the plot. Where there is more Bible background than you need, switch back to the action. The outlying puzzle pieces will make more sense after you have glimpsed the big picture of how it all fits together. You can come back later for seconds, to chew on the contents or characters that intrigue you or strike a chord in your own story.

To make each **Backstory** more relevant and practical, two short sections may follow. These can awaken your memories and rouse your reactions to tough times in your life. **Bottomed Out** could evoke memories of painful or perplexing times when the bottom fell out on you. Even if you have recovered and moved on from them, reviewing and renewing them can encourage you by how you have survived them. Or this may reveal there is still some work to be done, a lesson to learn, or a healing to be had.

Battle Back can help you start to move forward again, put the pieces of your life back together, and start making progress. From childhood days, you may remember a large, inflatable toy, weighted at the bottom, tapering to the top, and painted to resemble a clown. However softly it was hit, it bent over. But no matter how hard it was slugged and bent backward, even parallel to the floor, it bounced right back to its upright position. Real people do not bounce back that quickly when the bottom falls out. It's a battle, and sometimes more like a war. Battles are tough and last longer than we expected. As Winston Churchill warned, they cost blood, sweat, and tears.

This is stressed in 2 Corinthians, the book for battlers. Its author Paul cites his own battles in 6:4–5 and chronicles his battle scars in 11:23–28. He cautions that believers are not exempt from the battles of life but calls us to be strong in the Lord to fight and win them. Be encouraged by these verses to keep battling:

We were so utterly burdened beyond our strength that we despaired of life itself … . We felt that we had received the sentence of death. But that was to make us rely not on ourselves but on God who raises the dead (2 Corinthians 1:8b–9).

But thanks be to God, who in Christ always leads us in triumphal procession (2:14).

Such is the confidence that we have through Christ toward God. Not that we are sufficient in ourselves to claim anything as coming from us, but our sufficiency is from God (3:4–5).

But we have this treasure in jars of clay, to show that the surpassing power belongs to God and not to us. We are afflicted in every way,

but not crushed; perplexed, but not driven to despair; persecuted,
but not forsaken; struck down, but not destroyed (4:7–9).

For though we walk in the flesh, we are not waging war according
to the flesh. For the weapons of our warfare are not of the flesh
but have divine power to destroy strongholds (10:3–4).

Part One's chapters with all the backstories will take the bulk of
this book. Part Two, "Victors: The Songs of the Sons of Korah," is much
shorter, like an epilogue. As we peruse their psalms in what seems to
be their chronological order, the realities behind their writings will
surface. Your figurative fulfillment of these truths will be emboldened
by how they lived them literally. Source Scriptures are teasers to begin
the chapters or noted in the play-by-play.

I predict this story will grab you, as it grabbed me. I pray that it will
grow you, as it has grown me. I petition that modern daughters and
sons of Korah will be steeled to say, "God is our refuge and our strength,
a very present help in trouble. Therefore we will not fear though the
earth gives way" (Psalm 46:1–2), and "I would rather be a doorkeeper in
the house of my God than dwell in the tents of wickedness. … For a day
in your courts is better than a thousand elsewhere" (Psalm 84:10b, 10a).

CHAPTER 2

SHOWDOWN AT SUNSET: KORAH, MOSES, AND AARON

And they rose up before Moses … . They assembled themselves together against Moses and against Aaron (Numbers 16:2–3).

When Moses heard this, he fell on his face; and he spoke to Korah and all his group, saying, "Tomorrow morning the LORD will make known who is His, and who is holy, and will bring that one near to Himself; indeed, the one whom He will choose, He will bring near to Himself" (Numbers 16:4–5, NASB).

"Tomorrow" is the signature song in the movie musical *Annie*. This title repeats sixteen times in its lyrics. Tomorrow is also the reverberating word in the minds of Moses and Korah as they part ways from their momentous meeting. But Broadway fiction could not erase the facts and factions hanging over their heads or the ones we face in real life.

Jesus said, "Enter through the narrow gate; for the gate is wide and the way is broad that leads to destruction, and there are many who enter through it. For the gate is narrow and the way is constricted that leads to life, and there are few who find it" (Matthew 7:13–14, NASB).

Anything unresolved in the present may come calling on us in the future. *Payday, Someday* is how R.G. Lee expressed it, as the title of his classic sermon. Reckoning awaits us sooner or later in this life or the next, with or without advance notice. Such was the scene in Numbers sixteen. There was not a long interval or interim on the front end. The problem came to a head one day and was headed for a solution the next.

> *Now Korah ... of Levi, and Dathan and Abiram ... and On ..., sons of Reuben, took men. And they rose up before Moses, with a number of the people of Israel, 250 chiefs of the congregation, chosen from the assembly, well-known men. They assembled themselves together against Moses and against Aaron and said to them, "You have gone too far! For all in the congregation are holy, every one of them, and the LORD is among them. Why then do you exalt yourselves above the assembly of the LORD?" (Numbers 16:1–3)*

None of Korah's conspirators named above are from his own tribe of Levi. He had already alienated them as his closest kin. Levi, a son of Abraham's grandson Jacob, had three sons himself: Gershon, Kohath, and Merari (Exodus 6:16). God favored Kohath, the grandfather of Moses, Aaron, and Korah. The Kohathites received better assignments (Numbers 4:1–20) than their cousins from Kohath's brothers, Gershon (4:21–28) and Merari (4:29–33).

Gershonites and Merarites could not be priests, but neither could Kohathites not descended from Moses' and Aaron's father, Amram. This excluded Korah from the priesthood and made him jealous of Aaron. But Korah had also lost out to another cousin, Uzziel's son Elizaphan, as head of all the Levites who were not priests (Numbers 3:29–30). As Korah licked his wounds, he coveted the priesthood, which would vault him above Elizaphan. Korah realized he could never be the High Priest. But he, Dathan, Abiram, and the 250 chiefs would press for a plurality of priests to allow that any Hebrew man who so desired could function in this role. Their charge, "you have gone too far," meant that by making the priesthood so exclusive, Moses and Aaron were elevating themselves above the nation.

More than twenty dozen leaders showed up for a showdown. They assembled together against Moses and Aaron. Their opening words were preemptive strikes, caustic and confrontational. Heads were going to roll. Just two, they expected: the heads of their heads, Moses and Aaron.

God had not run it by Korah when He chose Moses to deliver the Hebrews from Egypt. Korah gave Moses full credit for this initiative. He blamed Moses, charging him with inventing or usurping this role. Korah was correct in his assertion that all the congregation was to be holy. God Himself had said this five times in Leviticus (11:44, 45; 19:2; 20:7, 26). God in His providence made a fresh pronouncement just two verses of Scripture before Korah's rebellion: "Be holy to your God" (Numbers 15:40).

Korah shows our human tendency toward selective memory. He remembered and relished these divine calls for all Israel to be holy. He had conveniently forgotten when God chartered a more exclusive holy club. What God said twice in Leviticus 21:6 that "they shall be holy" to their God and the next verse that "he is holy to his God," He spoke not of every Israelite or even each Levite, but just the priests. "And the LORD said to Moses, 'Speak to the priests, the sons of Aaron, and say to them ...'" (Leviticus 21:1). Leviticus 21:7 states it clearly: "For the priest is holy to his God."

Korah himself was privilege to an inner circle of holiness, the Levites (all the male offspring of Jacob's son Levi). His covetous jealousy of a yet inner circle, which excluded him but included Aaron, boiled over and spewed its venom at Moses.

> *And Moses said to Korah, "Hear now, you sons of Levi: is it too small a thing for you that the God of Israel has separated you from the congregation of Israel, to bring you near to himself, to do service in the tabernacle of the* LORD *and to stand before the congregation to minister to them, and that he has brought you near him, and all your brothers the sons of Levi with you? And would you seek the priesthood also? Therefore it is against the* LORD *that you and all your company have gathered together. What is Aaron that you grumble against him?" (Numbers 16: 8–11).*

Challenges to the top rarely come from outside the ranks of leadership. They usually come from insiders, those close enough to observe the leaders in action and pick their faults. Secondary leaders have enough going for them to have gotten where they are. They may see the primary leader as the roadblock to their further ascent. The ultimate leader is most susceptible to grenades lobbed by a leader who is penultimate, whose pent-up jealousy finally erupts. The evil one we know as Satan was created as Lucifer. He was not content to be God's top angel; he wanted to be God himself (Isaiah 14:12–15; Ezekiel 28:13–17). A pastor's chief critic is often an entrenched deacon.

Korah had rolled the dice. The die was cast. The bottom would fall out on somebody, Moses and Aaron, or himself. From every human perspective and probability, Korah's *coup d'etat* was a *coup d'grace*, a done deal. But Moses was not done dealing. Verse 4 took longer in the sequence than it does in the sentence: "When Moses heard it, he fell on his face" (Numbers 16:4).

Moses fell on his face in despair. He had not wanted this job in the first place (Exodus 3:11; 4:10). There had been setbacks in Egypt and since Egypt. It had been an up-and-down process the whole way.

But since ten of the twelve spies had recommended that Canaan was a no-go (Numbers 13:28–33) and the congregation accepted the majority report, the wheels were coming off. The people grumbled against Moses and Aaron (14:2) and said, "Let us choose a leader and go back to Egypt" (14:4).

This call entered Korah's ears, and it stuck in his mind. Behind the scenes, he began offering his alternative leadership to any and all who griped about the incumbent. God pronounced a forty-year death sentence on everyone over twenty except Caleb and Joshua, the minority-report spies. Since Korah was thus doomed to die in this wilderness, he had little to lose.

The people had a change of heart overnight. By the next morning they were ready to charge into the Promised Land. But their window of opportunity had closed, just as we never know whether and how long the Lord will wait for us to obey. Moses warned them that it was too late, but they charged ahead, minus Moses and without the Lord's presence and blessing. The result was a disaster (Numbers 14:40–45).

The day before the showdown at sunup, Moses fell on his face to pray. We do not know what he prayed or if he prayed aloud. We do not know how long he prayed. He prayed long enough that some of his critics (the Reubenites) got tired of waiting for his answer and went home. He prayed long enough to receive an answer from the Lord and the holy boldness to face his foes. After prostrating himself to pour out his heart to God, Moses stood and spoke out with confidence and a clear plan. He received and relayed this protracted prayer's answer the same day:

And he spoke to Korah and all his group, saying, "Tomorrow morning the LORD will make known who is His, and who is holy, and will bring that one near to Himself; indeed, the one whom He will choose, He will bring near to Himself. Do this: take censers for yourselves, Korah and your whole group, and put fire in them, and place incense upon them in the presence of the LORD tomorrow; and the man whom the LORD chooses shall be the one who is holy. You have gone far enough, you sons of Levi!" (Numbers 16:5–7, NASB).

Moses got the militants' message loud and clear. Even Korah's exact words had stuck with him. Korah's charge against Moses and Aaron was: "You have gone far enough." Moses' booming voice boomeranged this back in Korah's face: "You have gone far enough, you sons of Levi." And Moses said to Korah, "You and all your company be present before the LORD tomorrow, both you and they along with Aaron" (Numbers 16:16, NASB).

There is a small but significant detail that played huge on this momentous day in Bible history, and Jewish writings note it. Their interpretation follows the main body of this backstory. Remember that the books of the Bible were not divided into chapters and verses until centuries after Jesus lived. When Moses wrote this as inspired Scripture, there was no break between Numbers 15:41 and 16:1, which starts and ends with "Korah … became insolent" (NIV).

Insolence is rude and disrespectful behavior. What triggered this in Korah? Probably the end of, and what was in, chapter 15. Chapter 14 was Israel's refusal to enter Canaan, which brought God's death sentence on all the adults but Caleb and Joshua (14:29–30). Chapter 15 begins with God talking about when the new generation will enter the land (15:2, 17). Verses 22–29 prescribe the offering for unintentional sins. The mood darkens when God offers no mercy for intentional sin:

" 'But anyone who sins defiantly, whether native-born or foreigner, blasphemes the LORD and must be cut off from the people of Israel. Because they have despised the LORD's word and broken his commands, they must surely be cut off; their guilt remains on them' " (Numbers 15:30–31, NIV).

Numbers 15:1–31 is actually one continuous direct quote from the Lord. Then something happens in the next two verses:

While the Israelites were in the wilderness, a man was found gathering wood on the Sabbath day. Those who found him gathering wood brought him to Moses and Aaron and the whole assembly, and they kept him in custody, because it was not clear what should be done to him (15:32–34, NIV).

We would quote the Fourth Commandment as "Remember the Sabbath day, to keep it holy." His peers who made a "citizen's arrest" thought he may not have, but the disposition was not clear. This would be a good debate subject for a youth or adult Sunday School class.

God had addressed this on three occasions. In the Ten Commandments, which God gave but Moses first delivered orally (Exodus 19:25), this Fourth Commandment is the longest — ninety-seven English words. Chapter 20:9 says to do all work in six days. Verse 10 says no work on the seventh day, which is a Sabbath to the Lord. Verse 11 says to do this because God, after creating the world in six days, rested on the seventh day, blessing the Sabbath day and making it holy.

Moses returned from another mountain visit with God with the Ten Tablets in stone to replace the original ones he broke at the golden calf incident.

Moses assembled the whole Israelite community and said to them,
"These are the things the LORD has commanded you to do: For six
days, work is to be done, but the seventh day shall be your holy
day, a day of sabbath to the LORD. Whoever does any work on it
is to be put to death. Do not light a fire in any of your dwellings
on the Sabbath day" (Exodus 35:1–3, NIV).

This was the **only** commandment on the agenda, as the next verse
launches five chapters on the materials and construction of the tabernacle.
So they knew this was a big deal with God. Three other details above are
pertinent to the question at hand: the whole assembly heard this, violation
draws a mandatory death sentence, and they were not to light a fire on the
Sabbath (which is probably why the man gathered the sticks).

Leviticus 23 is forty-three verses on the seven annual feasts of the
Lord, plus a single verse on the weekly Sabbath day: "There are six days
when you may work, but the seventh day is a day of sabbath rest, a day
of sacred assembly. You are not to do any work; wherever you live, it is
a sabbath to the LORD" (v. 3, NIV). Now back to the Sabbath day wood
gatherer: "Then the LORD said to Moses, 'The man must die. The whole
assembly must stone him outside the camp.' So the assembly took him
outside the camp and stoned him to death, as the LORD commanded
Moses" (Numbers 15:35–36, NIV).

The Lord's modus operandi was to tell Moses what to tell the people
(e.g. Numbers 15:1–2, 17–18, 35, 37). It had always worked this way,
whether in Egypt or here in the wilderness. The people of Israel in
general seemed to accept this (35–36). But they had to accept this by
faith, trusting God and Moses. Korah did not. He did not give Moses
the benefit of the doubt. He charged Moses with making up everything
for his own pleasure, power, and glory.

Our Jewish friends say the last passage in Numbers 15 (verses

37–41) was the last straw for Korah. Our Bible does not inform us if and how long there was a time gap before Korah's crew confronted Moses. The tassels below seem trivial to us (like name badges at work, or masks during Covid), but they were a big deal in Korah's mind.

> The LORD said to Moses, "Speak to the Israelites and say to them: 'Throughout the generations to come you are to make tassels on the corners of your garments, with a blue cord on each tassel. You will have these tassels to look at and so you will remember all the commands of the LORD, that you may obey them and not prostitute yourselves by chasing after the lusts of your own hearts and eyes. Then you will remember to obey all my commands and will be consecrated to your God. I am the LORD your God, who brought you out of Egypt to be your God. I am the LORD your God'" (Numbers 15:37–41, NIV).

The tassel's purpose in the passage above is a memory aid, like tying a string around a finger to help us remember something. The Bible mentions tassels or fringes seven times. The three times above are *tsitsith*, Hebrew for "fringe" or "lock (of hair)." The hair would be sheep hair or wool. Deuteronomy 22:12 uses *gedilim*, the Hebrew plural for "fringes" or "wreaths." The New International Version says, "Make tassels on the four corners of the cloak you wear," while the English Standard Version reads, "You shall make yourself tassels on the four corners of the garment with which you cover yourself."

The Synoptic Gospels use *kraspedon*, Greek for "tassel, fringe, extremity." The King James Version translates it as "border." Matthew, whose target audience was Jewish, has Jesus use the word to criticize the outward show and self-righteousness of the scribes and Pharisees: "They do all their deeds to be seen by others. For they make their phylacteries broad and their fringes long" (23:5).

The fringes themselves were not wrong, because God had commanded them. As an obedient Jewish man, Jesus wore them.

And wherever he came, in villages, cities, or countryside, they laid the sick in the marketplaces and implored him that they might touch even the fringe of his garment. And as many as touched it were made well (Mark 6:56).

When Jesus was on the way to raise Jairus' daughter from death, we read the following:

As Jesus went, the people pressed around him. And there was a woman who had had a discharge of blood for twelve years, and though she had spent all her living on physicians, she could not be healed by anyone. She came up behind him and touched the fringe of his garment, and immediately her discharge of blood ceased. And Jesus said, "Who was it that touched me?" When all denied it, Peter said, "Master, the crowds surround you and are pressing in on you!" But Jesus said, "Someone touched me, for I perceive that power has gone out from me." And when the woman saw that she was not hidden, she came trembling, and falling down before him declared in the presence of all the people why she had touched him, and how she had been immediately healed. And he said to her, "Daughter, your faith has made you well; go in peace" (Luke 8:42b–48).

The bottom had been fallen out on this woman for twelve years. Did you realize that these fringes that rescued this poor woman from a dozen years of suffering, and that were the means of healing for the countless cripples and chronically sick, were instituted by God in the verses immediately before Korah's revolt? These people were so thankful that Jesus did not protest them, as Korah did, but humbly submitted to their divine purpose.

We should not be content to remain on the fringes of serving God or communing with Him. "Seek ye first the kingdom of God" (Matthew 6:33, KJV). "But one thing I do: forgetting what lies behind and straining forward to what lies ahead, I press on toward the goal for the upward call of God in Christ Jesus" (Philippians 3:13–14). But isn't it great to know, like the woman in Luke 8, that if we can but touch the fringe of Jesus' garment, we can battle back in His life-changing power?

This day had started, and progressed, like any other day until Moses glimpsed a crowd of men headed his way. He had not summoned the congregation or the tribal leaders. Something was up! What? Moses made a quick prayer call. Hebrew men prayed standing with their heads tilted heavenward and their hands extended palms up. They left their eyes open as they looked to Yahweh. But this time, Moses was peeking, one eye on the crowd, which was getting closer. "Lord, help!"

As Korah's crowd drew nearer, Moses caught a visual detail out of the corner of his eye. His pulse jumped, and his heart raced. Korah had been nitpicking about the *techelet*, a wool string dyed blue-purple. He tried to undermine Moses by pointing to laws Korah viewed as illogical. He had begun by focusing on the *mitzvah of tzitzit*, the commandment to attach strings to the corners of one's garment, one of which should ideally be of wool dyed blue-purple.

Korah had prepared 250 cloaks without *tzitzit*, but which themselves were fashioned from wool dyed similarly and handed them to his supporters. To Moses, these 250 blue cloaks were like the uniforms of an enemy army marching to battle. As they lined up in Moses' face, too close for comfort, everyone within eyesight could hear a pin drop. Moses and Aaron stood speechless. Korah was the first to break the silence. His question to Moses was not rhetorical: "Do these cloaks require *tzitzit*?" Moses replied, "Yes, they do." Korah's crowd began to mock. Then Korah threw down the gauntlet. "For a garment of another color, one dyed wool string is sufficient, yet when an entire garment is dyed, its very color is not sufficient?" The opening salvo had been fired. A whole lot more than the sun would come out, tomorrow. The bottom would fall out ... on somebody ("Of Blue Threads and Doorposts" at www.chabad.org/library/article-cdo/aid/246641/jewish/Korah-the-Rebel-of-the-Bible.htm).

(*See Appendices in back for a brief summary of how God set apart the Levites as His special tribe.)

(Note to Reader)

This and succeeding chapters tell the saga of the sons of Korah. Each highlights an event, group, or character in this true story. This is the information. Such backstory may be followed by some optional application, which may begin with a theme.

The application steps may be used for individual reflection or group discussion.

Bottomed Out will help the reader or group member recall and relate incidents in which the bottom fell out. Start with a brief summary of what happened. Identify the feelings and emotions it triggered. Move to the consequences it caused, and end with any lingering symptoms.

Battling Back overviews how the victim can begin to recover. It highlights actions which could move this process forward. It will note areas that may need further remediation and suggest helpful steps. Outside resources may be recommended.

Blindsided

Sports movies rarely draw the general public to cinemas, but a 2009 football movie had a $309.2 million box office. Many recall it as a Sandra Bullock movie, which won her the Academy Award for Best Actress in a Leading Role.

The Blind Side is the true story of Michael Oher, a homeless African American teen who drifted in and out of the Eads, Tennessee, school system. Bullock played Leigh Anne Tuohy, who, with her husband Sean, took Michael in and became his legal guardian. With help from his new family and a good tutor, Oher realized his potential as a high school student and football player. He was an All-American at Ole Miss, a first-round NFL draft choice in 2009, and a Super Bowl winner in 2013.

Oher's huge frame and protective instincts fitted him for the offensive line's most strategic position: left tackle. Most quarterbacks are right-handed, so when they set up to pass, they are facing right and cannot see opposing defenders rushing from their left side. Most QB fumbles come when they are sacked from behind, when the blind side tackle fails to protect him. Oher won the Jacobs Trophy as the best blocker in college football because so few rushers were able to penetrate his QB's blind side.

In the hard knocks of life, we never know when something will come out of the blind side to knock us for a loop. It may sack our finances, threaten the life of a loved one, ruin a relationship, or cause pain and strain in other ways. We never know when the bottom may fall out on us.

Bottomed Out

One lady bared her soul on being blindsided. A family member and a close friend both died in the month she was diagnosed with potentially life-threatening cancer. The cancer proved benign, but its removal left a conspicuous scar. The bereavement, anxiety, and discouragement immobilized her for weeks — physically, mentally, and emotionally. What events in your life have bottomed you out the most?

Battling Back

Thinking about Jesus was the one thing that enabled her to begin to battle back. She began repeating His name aloud several times, focusing on Him for a moment. Meditating on Jesus kept her going, and it could for you. The book of Hebrews was written to Jewish-background Christians, being persecuted by non-Christian Jews. Their fellow messianic friend challenged them:

> Let us run with endurance the race that is set before us, looking to Jesus, the founder and perfecter of our faith … . Consider him who endured from sinners such hostility against himself, so that you may not grow weary or fainthearted (Hebrews 12:1b–3).

You've heard of deep breathing exercises. Think on Jesus as you do them. Paul wrote, "And whatever you do, in word or deed, do everything in the name of the Lord Jesus, giving thanks to God the Father through him" (Colossians 3:17). Doing this helped our above victim become a victor.

Think of this oxygen intake as inhaling God's peace. Then breathe out your anxiety. Repeat this until it calms your heart and mind. It may be helpful to journal your thoughts and feelings as you do this.

Beth experienced this after her healthy husband was blindsided by a cancer diagnosis, and a few months later died far too young. She reports, "In the days after his death, my mantra/prayer to our heavenly Father was 'I trust You, I trust You, I trust You.'" Something her husband had said gave her the faith to keep going: "We don't see everything we know. We don't know everything we see. But He sees and knows everything" (Tillman Cuttino Jr.). When others may have fallen apart, the Colossians 1:17 picture of Jesus became one of Beth's life verses: "He is before all things, and in Him all things hold together."

Read the book of Philippians during such times. It is practical, uplifting, and easy to understand. Read aloud a chapter a day, and you read the whole book in four days! Its author was in prison facing execution for sharing his faith, yet he said "joy" or "rejoice" sixteen times in four chapters. The key to joy is our mindset. He uses words like *think, mind, learn, know, trust, agree, convinced, count, consider,* or *remember* twenty-six times. You cannot control what happens to you, but you can control how you learn and grow from it.

Paul wrote, "The Lord is at hand; do not be anxious about anything, but in everything by prayer and supplication with thanksgiving let your requests be made known to God. And the peace of God, which surpasses all understanding, will guard your hearts and your minds in Christ Jesus" (Philippians 4:5b–7).

Other resources will be suggested in my pages to follow. In the early days of your battling back, online helps may be more helpful in your thought process about your situation. Friends and loved ones can help you emotionally and provide comfort and a sounding board by their presence.

When the bottom falls out on us because we have been blindsided, we may be so floored or flustered that we are too psychologically paralyzed to know what help we need. But don't go it alone. From her experience in giving and receiving help, Ginger urges, "Don't be afraid to ask others for help. Don't deprive them of the blessing of serving someone with a need."

If you are too shy or introverted to take the initiative to ask for help, at least be open to the helpers the Lord sends your way. If you think you don't need the specific way they offer to help, thank them and say that it may be helpful later. If there is something different you really need now, post it as a prayer request or share it with people near you. They may know of someone else who could render such assistance and may be willing to provide it.

Be praying these specifics for yourself! "More things are wrought by prayer than this world dreams of" (Tennyson, *Idylls of the King*). As the sons of Korah wrote in sacred Scripture, "God is our refuge and strength, a very present help in trouble" (Psalm 46:1).

CHAPTER 3

MR. IDENTITY CRISIS: MOSES

Moses' fourth recorded statement in Scripture is life's most basic question: "Who am I?" (Exodus 3:11). This question haunted him his whole life. Does it ever visit you?

Identity crisis is a period of uncertainty and confusion in which a person's sense of identity becomes insecure, typically due to a change in their expected aims or role in society. Moses lived thousands of years before German psychiatrist Erik Erikson coined the term, but Moses showed the symptoms of Identity Cohesion versus Role Confusion.

In this tension for Moses, there were spikes of identity cohesion, but stints of role confusion. Moses' expected aims and roles experienced two major upheavals in his vocational career, besides family relationships, economic status, geographical location, and his acceptance or rejection by his peers or followers.

Moses' identity crisis was not just psychological, but sociological. He was born a Hebrew but raised Egyptian when the Hebrews were Egypt's worst immigration nightmare. He was both, but neither. He spoke Egyptian with a Hebrew accent and Hebrew with an Egyptian accent.

To further muddy the waters, he lived midlife as a Midianite. When his first child was born in Midian, Moses shoehorned his identity crisis into the boy's name: "One son was named Gershom, for Moses said, 'I have become a foreigner in a foreign land'" (Exodus 18:3, NIV).

The three episodes of his life made Moses trilingual. He learned three languages, but he was never comfortable speaking any of them. Problem pronunciations accentuated his accent and shouted that he was an outsider. So, he was a man of few words, the strong silent type. He rarely spoke and, even when he did, was often the worst for it.

Moses was more Egyptian than Hebrew in his communication choice. He chose writing over speaking. Part of this comfort was cultural. Egyptians were proud of their hieroglyphics, which gave them superiority over other nations, most of which would still be oral cultures for centuries. Growing up in a world-class educational system, Moses learned to read and write hieroglyphics, which became the vehicle for state-of-the-art learning in every other field. Moses' home was the palace, where the only voice that mattered was Pharaoh's. Its worst-case scenario was for anyone to say something that contradicted the Pharaoh, so Moses played it safe and silent.

Psalm 45:1 could have been a good life verse for Moses: "My tongue is like the pen of a ready scribe." It would be written decades later by the sons of Korah. Moses himself would become the human author of the Bible's first five books (the Pentateuch or *Torah*) and the ninetieth psalm. So Moses wrote many times more Scripture than he spoke.

Moses' strongest and most specific reservation in answering God's call at the burning bush was being speech-challenged: "O, my Lord, I am not eloquent, either in the past or since you have spoken to your servant, but I am slow of speech and of tongue" (Exodus 4:10). God spoke to him there in Hebrew, so he understood and could reply, but Moses had felt no supernatural surge in his speaking ability or ease. This was not a lame excuse Moses was giving. He was aware of and actually describing the brain-processing loop required before his vocal cords could say anything.

People may speak multiple languages, but there is one of them in which they think. Usually this is their heart language or mother tongue

— the one heard on their mother's knee. Heart language is usually set by age three. When spoken to in another language, the brain translates this into heart language, which decides how to reply. Then the brain must translate this back into the secondary language, which the mouth will use to reply to the other person.

When Jochebed had weaned Moses and returned her son to Pharaoh's daughter (Exodus 2:7–10), Hebrew was the heart language fixed in his brain. But he would function in an Egyptian-speaking household for the next thirty-seven years, then a Midianite-speaking world for four more decades. By the time he was thrust back into a Hebrew-speaking situation, his brain was eighty years old. He would write in Psalm 90:10 that our physical functions start to decline at age seventy.

The Bible details Moses' birth and preschool years but records just six words he said his first four decades of life (Exodus 2:13). Scripture skips over three dozen years for Moses. When it finally breaks its silence on Moses, his question draws one in return by a Hebrew slave (Exodus 2:14). Moses' answer is not to reply, but to run. The basic human reactions to conflict are fight or flight. Moses could run away quicker than he could decide what to say. But this runaway became one of the most famous figures in world history.

Tourists may run into three Moses' sculptures in Washington, DC. One stands in the main reading room at the Library of Congress. Another sits, holding the Ten Commandments as the central figure on the Supreme Court's east exterior. The one standing at the Smithsonian has two horns on the head, a tribute to Michelangelo's mammoth marble masterpiece at St. Peter's Basilica in Rome.

We read in Exodus 34 that Moses' face would shine after he had been in God's presence, reflecting God's glory. The Hebrew words for "glory" and "horns" are very similar, so Jerome chose the latter when he translated the Latin Vulgate. This was the Bible used in Michelangelo's medieval Catholic Italy, so he sculpted horns on Moses' head. He softened this slap by sculpting Moses so large that the horns are not visible to viewers from floor level.

Sigmund Freud, founder of psychoanalysis, spent three weeks studying the emotional effects of Michelangelo's *Moses*. He describes Moses in a complex emotional state. Moses would begrudgingly agree. Korah would have said "Amen" to Freud's diagnosis and Michelangelo's depiction. Throughout history, leaders are viewed as larger than life. They are glorified or demonized, as we see today in a polarized United States.

Even good things, like this glory, exacerbated Moses' identity crisis. Having been in God's literal presence for days on end, his facial skin absorbed and reflected the gleam of God's glory. He was not aware of this until its first impression on his fellow Israelites, but the afterglow of God's glory stayed on his face for days. It was so bright that it freaked out his peers, as if he were radioactive. Sunglasses had not been invented yet, so Moses veiled his face while it still shone (Exodus 34:29–35).

This glorious glow was so glaring that Paul mentioned it a millennium later: "with such glory that the Israelites could not gaze at Moses' face because of its glory" (2 Corinthians 3:7). This led to Moses keeping the veil on too long, to hide the fact that the glow had worn off (evidence that it had been a while since he had been with God). "Not like Moses, who would put a veil over his face so that the Israelites might not gaze at the outcome of what was being brought to an end" (2 Corinthians 3:13).

This godly glow has touched New Testament believers through Jesus. "For God, who said, 'Let light shine out of darkness,' has shone in our hearts to give the light of the knowledge of the glory of God in the face of Jesus Christ" (2 Corinthians 4:6). Jesus said, "You are the light of the world ... . Let your light shine before others, so that they may see your good works and give glory to your Father who is in heaven" (Matthew 5:14, 16). When we have been with Jesus, others notice His reflection in our lives. "Now when they saw the boldness of Peter and John, and perceived that they were uneducated, common men, they were astonished. And they recognized that they had been with Jesus" (Acts 4:13).

Once this difference has distinguished us, we are on the horns of a dilemma when we slip back into our old ways. We will be tempted to fake it, like Moses' veil when it was no longer needed to shield, but he kept it on to hide. We can cover up and pretend, or we can confess our sins to be covered by Christ and restore the joy of our salvation.

Moses' psychological complexity surfaced at the pressure points in the desert. He had enough covenant consciousness to know circumcision was its sign. As far ahead into the Scripture story as Acts 15, even Christian Jews would still be linking circumcision with Moses: "Some men came down from Judea and were teaching the brothers, 'Unless you are circumcised according to the custom of Moses, you cannot be saved'" (Acts 15:1). But Moses was heading out to help deliver the Hebrews without having delivered his own sons from their foreskins (Exodus 4:24–26). Later he begged off the assignment twice, telling God his own lips were uncircumcised (Exodus 6:12, 30). These uncircumcised lips would sometimes let slip something very discordant with the covenant.

Moses was at his best when he did not let complaints stick to him when he knew they were really directed at God. "What are we? Your grumbling is not against us but against the LORD" (Exodus 16:8). "Therefore the people quarreled with Moses and said, 'Give us water to drink.' And Moses said to them, 'Why do you quarrel with me? Why do you test the LORD?'" (Exodus 17:2).

Moses' identity crisis could confuse him as to who was delivering the Hebrew people from slavery in Egypt to Promised Land prosperity. Was it the Lord? Or was it Moses? The Hebrews' complaining challenged the patience of their leaders, human and divine.

Their gripes were hard to hold for Moses or even for the God of grace. The golden calf incident pushed God's patience to the limit, and, for a brief moment, He disowned them. "And the LORD said to Moses, 'Go down, for your people, whom you brought up out of the land of Egypt, have corrupted themselves'" (Exodus 32:7). In this rare instance, Moses' patience and grace exceeded even God's. The Lord is ready to wipe out this corporate people and reset Abraham's blessing onto Moses and his progeny. But Moses intervenes and intercedes, and "the LORD relented from the disaster that he had spoken of bringing on his people" (Exodus 32:14).

Moses' worst manifested in Numbers 11. The people started complaining again, murmuring about the manna in particular. They had grown weary of their boring diet. And Moses was tired of them.

Moses heard the people weeping throughout their clans, everyone at the door of his tent. And the anger of the LORD blazed hotly, and Moses was displeased. Moses said to the LORD, "Why have you dealt ill with your servant? And why have I not found favor in your sight, that you lay the burden of all this people on me? Did I conceive all this people? Did I give them birth, that you should say to me, 'Carry them in your bosom, as a nurse carries a nursing child,' to the land that you swore to give their fathers? Where am I to get meat to give to all this people? For they weep before me and say, 'Give us meat, that we may eat.' I am not able to carry all this people alone; the burden is too heavy for me. If you will treat me like this, kill me at once, if I find favor in your sight, that I may not see my wretchedness" (Numbers 11:10–15).

This group griping would finally get Moses' goat and his number in Numbers 20 at Kadesh, where God had the people stay much longer than planned. The chapter begins with the death of Miriam. Even as Moses and Aaron start to grieve their only sister, the people blame them for no drinking water. "Why have you brought the assembly of the LORD into this wilderness, that we should die here, both we and our cattle? And why have you made us come up out of Egypt to bring us to this evil place?" (Numbers 20:4–5).

The people finally bring Moses down to their level. In a moment of weakness, perhaps in the grasp of grief's shock and numbness, he parrots their humanistic theology. He accepts the level of credit and responsibility that God alone could shoulder.

Recognizing thirst as His people's legitimate but pressing need and wanting to confirm both Moses' leadership and God's divine provision, the Lord is unwilling to let their bad disposition preclude His good provision. He tells Moses to speak to the rock, and water will flow. But Moses' hot head hardens his hearing. He misses God's tweak in technique (tell the rock, not strike). He reverts to past procedure for getting water to flow from solid stone:

> *Then Moses and Aaron gathered the assembly together before the rock, and he said to them, "Hear now, you rebels: shall we bring water for you out of this rock?" And Moses lifted up his hand and struck the rock with his staff twice, and water came out abundantly, and the congregation drank, and their livestock. And the LORD said to Moses and Aaron, "Because you did not believe in me, to uphold me as holy in the eyes of the people of Israel, therefore you shall not bring this assembly into the land that I have given them." These are the waters of Meribah, where the people of Israel quarreled with the LORD, and through them*

he showed himself holy (Numbers 20:10–13).

This passage gives pause to casual Bible readers, provoking two questions: How could the Lord be hallowed among this griping group, in an incident which brings Moses the most severe sentence of his sojourn on earth, and since God met Moses' aim and the people's need by producing water from the rock, why does God punish Moses so severely by banning him from entering the Promised Land?

(1) The people came way short of hallowing the Lord in this incident, in their intentions, attitude, statements, or actions. They were anything but holy. But in God's sovereignty, He gets praise out of even the wrath of man (Psalm 76:10).

The Lord's positive attributes are almost countless, but His greatest is holiness. It is His singular trait that the Bible trumpets in triplicate. Since God's Word requires any truth to be confirmed by two or three witnesses (Deuteronomy 17:6; Matthew 18:16b; 2 Corinthians 13:1b), God uses the plural *seraphim* as the Old Testament witnesses, "Holy, holy, holy is the LORD of Hosts" (Isaiah 6:3), and with "the four living creatures" as the New Testament clarions: "Holy, holy, holy, is the Lord God Almighty" (Revelation 4:8). The Hebrew language of the Old Testament lacks the comparative and superlative tenses, so this "three-peat" is the Hebrew equivalent for "holiest."

Holy is God's summary synonym, as it sums up the perfection of all His other attributes. Holy means "unique" or "other" because of being "different from" and "better than." God told Moses to speak to the rock, but he disobeyed God's command by striking the rock. He devalued God's character by handling the situation like a mad man, instead of a loving God.

(2) In an unfortunate parallel to the triple trumpeting of God's holiness, Moses is guilty of a threefold trampling of it. First, he commits

a transgression, a disobedience to a specific command. God said speak to the rock, but Moses struck it, instead. Second, he sinned. "For all have sinned and fall short of the glory of God" (Romans 3:23). "Whatever does not proceed from faith is sin" (Romans 14:23). The Lord said this was an act of not believing God, and it robbed the Lord of glory due Him. Third, Moses violated a type or prophetic picture of Christ. First Corinthians 10:1–11 cites this period of biblical history, twice stating that its events in general are examples for us. A few of these Old Testament events are also types, which prefigure and point to New Testament realities.

For example, their passing through the Red Sea was a type of New Testament baptism. The rock from which they drank water when Moses struck it was a type of Christ. "For they drank from the spiritual Rock that followed them, and the Rock was Christ" (1 Corinthians 10:4). Because Jesus' once-for-all-time death on the cross was sufficient to save anyone who believes, He does not need to die again. Since the Rock was Christ, symbolically, Moses did not have to strike it again to get water. By doing so, Moses violated the type, implying that Christ's death did not accomplish everything. But Jesus said on the cross that it did: "It is finished" (John 19:30b). Several New Testament passages warn against the impossibility of Christ needing to die a second time since He had done this once for all (Romans 6:10; Hebrews 6:6; 7:27; 9:12, 26, 28; 10:10, 12, 14).

Losing his temper so badly that he struck the rock was uncharacteristic of Moses, despite the isolated instances when his anger erupted. Meekness is strength under control. After Moses had finished writing the book of Numbers, the Holy Spirit inspired someone (probably Joshua, who would have recorded Moses' death in the last chapter of Deuteronomy) to add an editorial comment to the text of Numbers. Most Bible versions show Numbers 12:3 in parentheses to note its insertion by a later writer: "Now Moses was a very humble man, more humble than anyone else on the face of the earth" (Numbers 12:3, NIV).

Moses' high-water mark was the triumphant song of praise he composed and led on the safe side of the Red Sea. "Then Moses and the people of Israel sang this song to the LORD" (Exodus 15:1). Its opening words are "I will sing to the LORD." Its nineteen verses never name or even allude to Moses as God's human agent in this victory, but he mentions God thirteen times. The Lord liked this song so much that He included it in the Bible and will reprise it in heaven.

> *Then I saw another sign in heaven, great and amazing, seven angels with seven plagues, which are the last, for with them the wrath of God is finished. And I saw what appeared to be a sea of glass mingled with fire — and also those who had conquered the beast and its image and the number of its name, standing beside the sea of glass with harps of God in their hands. And they sing the song of Moses, the servant of God, and the song of the Lamb, saying, "Great and amazing are your deeds, O Lord God the Almighty! Just and true are your ways, O King of the nations! Who will not fear, O Lord, and glorify your name? For you alone are holy. All nations will come and worship you, for your righteous acts have been revealed" (Revelation 15:1–4).*

Backstory

Even spiritual superstars like Moses got bottomed out. His nemeses were fear, failure, rejection, and upheaval. These villains often traveled together and visited Moses.

> *One day, when Moses had grown up, he went out to his people and looked on their burdens, and he saw an Egyptian beating*

a Hebrew, one of his people. He looked this way and that, and seeing no one, he struck down the Egyptian and hid him in the sand. When he went out the next day, behold, two Hebrews were struggling together. And he said to the man in the wrong, "Why do you strike your companion?" He answered, "Who made you a prince and a judge over us? Do you mean to kill me as you killed the Egyptian?" Then Moses was afraid, and thought, "Surely the thing is known." When Pharaoh heard of it, he sought to kill Moses. But Moses fled from Pharaoh and stayed in the land of Midian (Exodus 2:11–15).

We can get bottomed out by the backfire of our good intentions. A middle school boy's dog followed him on a visit to his best friend, who also had a dog. The boys were friends, but their dogs were not and began fighting. When the visitor reached in to break up the dogfight, his own dog bit him.

The New Testament commends Moses for the faith that underlay his motivation when he tried to play the role of peacemaker.

By faith Moses, when he was grown up, refused to be called the son of Pharaoh's daughter, choosing rather to be mistreated with the people of God … . By faith he left Egypt, not being afraid of the anger of the king, for he endured as seeing him who is invisible (Hebrews 11:24–27).

After thirty-seven years of regal rearing, Moses had put two and two together to conclude that his Hebrew and Egyptian identities would converge into conflict. He had long prayed for God to set his people free from their cruel slavery. But the more he prayed, the less he could see a solution where he was just a spectator. Moses knew their deliverance was the "what" of God's will. He suspected that he might be the "who." But he was way off on the "how" and the "when." Moses got ahead of the Lord, as we are prone to do.

Two pieces of God's plan were missing. There were still forty years left on the grace period God was giving the Amorites (Genesis 15:13–16). Then, He would be just and righteous in using the invading Hebrews to execute His death sentence on this cruel, carnal gateway people group of the land of Canaan. And Moses himself would need these forty years to intern as a shepherd in the same wilderness where he would shepherd the children of Israel for four decades.

Those would be good years for him. Moses would meet and marry his life partner, experience the joy of parenting, and enjoy the peace and quiet of being just a normal guy. But this hiatus was bookended by major upheavals, out of and back into Egypt, both under pressure. His tormentors fear and failure found him both times and tag-teamed to wrestle him as fear of failure.

Moses' worst fear was rejection. He was quickly rejected the first time he tried to rescue just one Hebrew. So the rejection fear skyrocketed when God would deploy him to deliver millions of them. Moses answered "here" when his name was called at the burning bush (Exodus 2:4). But it went downhill from there. He was afraid to look at God (2:6). His first words after God's call were, "Who am I that I should go to Pharaoh and bring the children of Israel out of Egypt?" (3:11). He moved the needle from "If I go" to "What if" (2:13), then was mute for the ten verses in the rest of the chapter while God overviewed the whole plan of how the mission would succeed.

Moses' fear of rejection and failure dismissed this out of hand. "But behold, they will not believe me or listen to my voice, for they will say, 'The LORD did not appear to you'" (Exodus 4:1).

So God gave him three miracle-working powers to bolster his faith

(Exodus 4:2–9), two to demonstrate on the spot and one to use at the Nile River. Moses rebuffed them, using his lack of oratory skills as an excuse (4:10–12), then declined the mission (4:12).

God often gives us what we ask for but to our detriment. When Moses said, "Oh, my Lord, please send someone else" (4:13), God gave in and sent his brother Aaron to assist him (4:14–16). But Aaron will turn out to be more of a hindrance than a help.

Bottomed Out

When and how did the bottom fall out on you in fear of failure, or rejection? Which of these is the biggest challenge in your life now? Is there one from your past that still haunts you? Is there one where the wound is so fresh or still so deep that it is difficult to admit to or share with someone?

Battling Back

When you think about all your fears, failures, and rejection, it is overwhelming and can be emotionally paralyzing. Pray for a few days for the Lord to show you which ones to just trust Him with for a while. Then, pray a specific prayer aloud, naming these things you are trusting Him with. Next, pray for God to show you which one to focus on now because you know one or two things you can do that will make some difference. Ask Him to give you the strength to act on this and to nudge you when to do this, within the next few days. Finally, identify one fear, failure, or rejection you are stumped on right now. Pray for the Lord to give you some insight on this week. Make a note of this insight when it comes and how to act on it.

CHAPTER 4

BAD BLOOD: KORAH

*And the L*ORD *spoke to Moses, saying, "Take the Levites from among the people of Israel and cleanse them. Thus you shall do to them to cleanse them: sprinkle the water of purification upon them, and let them go with a razor over all their body, and wash their clothes and cleanse themselves" (Numbers 8:5–7).*

Whenever Korah heard his name, it was the Hebrew word "baldness." To call him by name was to call him "Baldy." It was a derisive term, especially for males whose hair turns loose before they turn old. Shaved heads are cool in some cultures, but that is baldness by decision.

Korah is also translated "ice, hail, or frost." So he was as cool then as shaved heads are now. Warmth was not his nature or personality. He was a cool customer with ice in his veins. Only a cool customer would go toe-to-toe with Moses. Korah was envious and jealous of Moses' long, flowing hair. As if he did not have reasons enough, already.

Korah's baldness was actually by Moses, or at least he blamed it on Moses. When the Lord instituted the Levites, His consecration protocol through Moses included shaving their whole bodies. Some males have little or no body hair, so the most conspicuous consecration consequence for such Levites was their shaved heads. At Korah's advanced age, the hair did not grow back on his head. Most of the Levites held their heads high for their spiritual significance. But under Korah's shaved head was a stiff neck. He did not like anyone telling him what to do or making him do it.

National or ethnic pride prompts many countries or peoples to sanitize and spruce up their histories and stories. They tone down, explain away, or omit the ignoble parts, vile villains, and awkward exploits. One reason we know Bible stories are true stories is that God's Word presents its characters warts and all, rather than edit out their foibles and failures.

The Korah stories to follow share details and quotes handed down orally from one generation to another, then eventually put into writing. (I explain these writings on pages 223-225.)

Korah's wife was rough about her husband's smooth head. "Cora" Korah would never forgive Moses for it. Korah had a head of hair when she married him, and she liked his hair and loathed its amputation:

"See what Moses has done. He has made thee shave all thy hair in order to disfigure thee," she said.

For once, Korah defended Moses. "But he has done the same to his own sons."

But that did not console cantankerous Cora, who countered, "Moses hated thee so much that he was ready to do evil to his own children provided the same evil would overtake thee" (Midrash Aggadah to Numbers 16:8; Yalkut Shimoni, Numbers 750; comp. Numbers Rabbah 1.c.: Tanakh1.c; Sanhedrin 110a).

The Jewish Talmud, in Sanhedrin 109b, offers a different explanation for Korah's name, "baldness:" It was given to him in retrospect on account of the "gap" or "blank," which he made in Israel by his revolt (death of 15,000 men, Numbers 16:35, 49). This seems anachronistic, as the name Korah is used consistently from the start of the historical narrative.

Korah's name appears first in Exodus 6:21 in a genealogical list. Genealogies look back, so they use a person's given name, the one they were given by their parents at birth, not one they may have earned later in life by their own deeds or misdeeds. The book of Exodus was written by Korah's contemporary, Moses. They were co-participants in the events recorded from Exodus 4:29 through Numbers 16:33. If the name Korah was an aftermath of the Numbers 16 incident, what was this person called in the fourscore years he actually lived? And why would his given name not have been used in reporting the events as he actually experienced them?

A Jewish apocryphal source names Korah as one of four Levites to carry the Ark of the Covenant on their shoulders each time the tabernacle was moved (Tanahk, ed. Buber, Korah, Supplement.5, Numbers Rabbah vviii.2). The Old Testament does not name them, which implies Korah was too old for this honor. He was a first cousin and contemporary of Aaron and Moses, who were eighty or older before the ark was built. The age for active Levite duty was thirty to fifty (Numbers 4:3, 23, 30, 35, 39, 43). Fifty sounds young for retirement, and twenty years seems short for a career. But twenty years has long earned retirement pay in the U.S. military, where many have begun drawing this in their early forties.

The Talmud also attributes great wealth to Korah, suggesting he discovered one of the treasures, which Joseph had hidden in Egypt (Joseph stored grain, Genesis 41:46–49, not "gain"). If there was a grain of truth in this, it could spark a theory that the 250 leaders joined in when Korah confronted Moses because he had bribed them. But this Talmud tale seems too tall as to be absurd, that it took three hundred mules to carry just the keys of Korah's treasures (Peshitta 119a; Sanhedrin 110a).

Since Korah and his Hebrew contemporaries were slaves until they departed Egypt in Exodus 12:51, it is highly unlikely he could have amassed, protected, managed, and moved such a sheer volume of treasure. There was just a four-day notice for the plans and preparations for the Passover that pulled the trigger on the exodus from Egypt. The Hebrew slaves would have still been working days, probably long ones. Tired slaves would have been hard pressed to round up three hundred mules in the three intervening nights, to load them to leave with such treasure.

The Bible account is that the Hebrews did leave with treasure as God blessed them with a lump-sum payment for their four centuries of slave labor. But this treasure was primarily precious metals made into jewelry, which would have been much easier to carry away, and appeared to have been somewhat equally distributed among the Hebrews (Exodus 12:35–36; 25:1–3, 7; 32:2–3; 35:4–5, 9; 36:2–7).

Since their fathers were brothers (Exodus 6:16–21), Moses was Korah's **first** cousin, sharing the same paternal grandfather, Kohath. (Since this branch of Levi's family tree included Korah, Moses, and the priests, this book will often mention the Kohathite third of the Levites.) Korah turned out to be Moses' **worst** cousin. His jealous, resentful envy traced back to Egyptian slavery, which Moses escaped, but Korah endured. Korah and Aaron were on the tail end of the Hebrew baby boom, the tipping point triggering Pharaoh's infanticide edict for Jewish babies born male. Hebrew girls were no problem, but boys might grow up to be soldiers drafted by an army invading Egypt.

Izhar's middle child, Nepheg (Hebrew for "sprout"), just beat the boy baby ban, so his life took root. But Izhar's baby boy was butchered. Zichri (Hebrew for "renown") did not sprout but stood out because he was snuffed out. Losing his little brother was grief enough for Korah. Grief grew from the fresh wound when Aaron's little brother, Moses, dodged the bullet.

Birth order traits exacerbated other differences that Korah and

Moses would have in the brief times their lives intertwined. Korah was a firstborn child; Moses, the baby of the family. Firstborns tend to be conscientious rule followers. Korah despised Pharaoh's death sentence on their boy babies, but as the law of the land, it had to be obeyed. Korah rationalized that their quick deaths would spare them a lifetime of hardship in Egyptian slavery and that their innocence on earth would spare them in the afterlife. He could not justify the disobedience and lies of the Hebrew midwives who defied the edict. They bought a bit more time for a few little boys, but the parents had to pay for it with interest. Korah was old enough to remember the surprise inspections at Goshen when squads of Egyptian soldiers would swoop in, raid all the tents, butcher any baby boys, and beat the guilty parents caught red handed in their defiant disobedience.

Korah's aunt and uncle, Jochebed and Amram, defied the edict and concocted a crazy plan. Their baby boat would not have survived the Nile crocodiles for long if Pharaoh's daughter had not retrieved it. Her ulterior motives outweighed any altruism or compassion. If she had children of her own womb, a Hebrew baby would have been a bother. But her younger brother's wife was now expecting their first child, who would become the uncontested heir to the throne. His older sister was Pharaoh's firstborn, but she was barren and running out of time for a preemptive strike. Her brother would contest the idea of an adopted heir.

So, when she took the infant out of the river and took him home, she took his name Moses from *Thutmose*, which three previous Pharaohs had used. But Moses sounds like the Hebrew word for "draw out" (Exodus 2:10), so God's providence gave Moses a Hebrew/Egyptian name, which would work when he was with either group. At least Moses would be the first grandson to sit on Pharaoh's lap and maybe the first to sit on his throne. She raised him in the palace, as an Egyptian.

Korah hoped he would never see Moses again. He tried to write him off, but he could not forgive Moses' parents, and he could not forget Moses. His favored, fortunate first cousin was out of sight but not out of mind. Korah could not let go. He would not let go.

It is interesting to contemplate what role(s) Korah may have had in the golden calf incident (Exodus 32) when Moses was delayed on the mountain with God. The Hebrews had never been allowed to see their God. Now it has been six weeks since they have seen their human leader. They pressure Aaron, in charge during Moses' absence, to make them gods they could see. Then, their idolatry morphed into immorality. Finally, Moses showed up when things were at their worst. Righteous indignation moved Moses to call for volunteers to restore order, and his fellow Levi tribesmen executed three thousand capital punishments.

In Numbers, which follows Exodus in the narrative, Korah emerges as discontent, so we could imagine him as complicit in the calf caper. But he was not in the thousands executed that day. The three thousand who died likely included the initiators who pressed Aaron for an idol, plus others who engaged in its licentious celebration. Exodus 32:26 says all the Levites rallied to Moses' crunch-time call as he drew the line in the sand: "Who is on the LORD's side? Come to me." So we must conclude that at this point in the narrative, Korah the Levite and his first cousin Moses were still on the same side.

Aaron's glaring failure that day was actually the crack in the dam. As the story proceeds, we see that Korah's resentment of the regime of Moses and especially Aaron came not from his own unrighteousness but from his self-righteousness. Korah would have maintained order that day and not let the people get out of hand, but Moses had not left him with the delegated authority to do so. Now that Aaron had stumbled, Korah would keep his eyes open for what Aaron would do, and his ears open for what Aaron might say. Aaron's feet of clay had been leaving footprints in the desert sand.

Betrayed

An Army officer arrived on March 1970 at the Iowa farm of Gene and Peg Mullen. He informed them that their son Michael had been killed in Vietnam. Those old enough to recall this unpopular war may have seen the 1979 Emmy-winning TV movie *Friendly Fire*, documenting the Mullen's determined attempts to learn more about the circumstances of their son's death. When they tried to learn how their son died, they met lies and evasions on all sides.

Friendly fire is an oxymoron, opposing words combined into a phrase that seems contradictory. Whoever coined the phrase probably never had a loved one wounded or killed by the misfire of someone supposedly on the same side. This all-too-familiar phrase is not just oxymoronic. Its compunction to classify whether friend or foe pulled the trigger pours salt in the wound, whether the victims survive or their loved ones mourn.

The margin for error in modern warfare makes a slight amount of friendly fire inevitable, one of the casualties of war. Friendly fire stings the hardest when it is intentional, not accidental. This blood-red scarlet thread is woven throughout human history. The first person ever born murdered the second one ever born (Cain and Abel, Genesis 4:1–8).

Assassinations spike this into public domain (e.g. Abraham Lincoln, John F. Kennedy, and Martin Luther King). Few assassins know their target personally or understand the complexities of governing a people or leading a movement. But when such friendly fire is intentional, literature perpetuates it, as William Shakespeare penned in *Julius Caesar*, Act 3, Scene 2:

> For Brutus, as you know, was Caesar's angel.
> Judge, O you gods, how dearly Caesar loved him!
> This was the most unkindest cut of all;
> For when the noble Caesar saw him stab,

Ingratitude, more strong than traitor's arms,

Quite vanquished him; then burst his mighty heart.

O what a fall was this, my countrymen!

Backstory

This chapter has the tragic story of someone who could not forgive. Korah could not forgive his first cousins Moses and Aaron, whom God had chosen over him as the governmental and religious leaders of the newly formed nation of Israel. He could not forgive Moses for living in luxury in Egypt's palace for thirty-seven years while Korah lived in a hut and did slave labor. He could not forgive Moses for running away to Midian for forty more years while Korah did four more decades of slave labor in Egypt. Moses had not paid his dues.

Korah could not forgive God for bringing Moses back as a hero instead of leaving him long forgotten in the desert. Korah could not forgive Moses for leaving brother Aaron in charge (instead of cousin Korah), while Moses ascended Mount Sinai to meet with God for who knows how long. He could also never forgive Aaron for letting the people run wild while Moses was gone. Korah would have maintained order, and not have let things get so out of hand. Korah especially could not forgive Aaron for making that golden calf, which made God and Moses mad, and ended up costing three thousand people their lives. He could not forgive Moses and Aaron that their own tribe of Levi had to be the ones to clean up the mess. The Levites would be forever resented by the descendants of the thousands of capital punishments they had to execute that fateful day.

Bottomed Out

Being blindsided is bad enough. When it comes from being betrayed, it is almost unbearable. Sometimes, people we know and love may have been complicit in it. This shock may be an aftershock, something we are told later or stumble across. In the times you recalled when the bottom fell out on you, was there an element of betrayal in any of them?

One area rife for betrayal is finances. Did someone borrow money from you, and never pay it back? Were you scammed? Did you lose thousands in the stock market because your broker or a friend gave you bad advice? Were you ripped off in a home improvement project or sold a car that was a lemon? Did you cosign a loan for someone and then were stuck paying it? The list goes on and on. We have all been burned. Consider how many of these burn marks still mar your memory.

When we said "I do," we subjected ourselves to the possibility of betrayals large or small. Half the couples marrying in the U.S. get divorced. Even when the divorce is "for the kids' sake," everyone involved in a divorce gets hurt. Some couples cite this as an excuse for just "living together." But cohabitating couples break up at a higher rate than married ones. Intact marriages are not exempt from betrayal. Affairs are unfair to the spouse, whose unforgiveness would be understandable.

Betrayal is in effect and hurts everyone in either family, whether or not they know, yet. Betrayal can be committed without leaving the house. Physical or verbal abuse, silent treatment, runaway spending, gambling debts, porn addiction, drug abuse, and other excesses betray the one who married "for better" but got the "or worse." Parents can feel betrayed by their children, especially teens or young adults, who have more opportunity to rebel in more expensive and embarrassing ways. When we are blindsided by those closest to us, it hurts the most. Recall the times you were blindsided by someone you love and for whom you have made so many sacrifices.

Jobs and careers are subject to being lost, betraying loyal employees. Companies are bought out, and workers are put out. Long-faithful employees are let go, because their benefits are too expensive, or their tech skills too dated. The COVID years closed businesses and cost jobs. Have you or a spouse lost a job you had found rewarding, both financially and in a sense of serving others? Had you been promised you could have that job for as long as you wanted? You felt betrayed if the rug was pulled out from under you.

Our health can betray us, as seniors discover in various ways. Injuries, diseases, and other health failures, ours or others, can betray us. We expect to live the life expectancy or beyond, but there are no guarantees. In what ways not mentioned above have you been betrayed?

Battling Back

When you are bottomed out by betrayal, the next nemesis to attack you will be unforgiveness. At first you may be too hurt to forgive. But unforgiveness will hurt you more. It is like your drinking poison but expecting it to kill whoever hurt you. The New Testament has much to say about forgiving others. One statement is the best known, because Jesus himself instructed us in the Sermon on the Mount and in the Lord's Prayer:

> *Pray then like this:*
> *"Our Father in heaven,*
> *hallowed be your name.*
> *Your kingdom come,*
> *your will be done,*
> *on earth as it is in heaven.*
> *Give us this day our daily bread,*
> *and forgive us our debts,*
> *as we also have forgiven our debtors.*
> *And lead us not into temptation,*
> *but deliver us from evil."*

For if you forgive others their trespasses, your heavenly Father will also forgive you, but if you do not forgive others their trespasses, neither will your Father forgive your trespasses (Matthew 6:9–15).

Is it our "trespasses" or our "debts" we need forgiven? The churches I grew up in said trespasses when we prayed this in unison. As I had occasion to visit other churches, I noticed that some of them said debts. Either one is appropriate. Debt is a financial term that involves monetary need, but not necessarily a moral or spiritual wrong. My tribe preferred trespasses, which implies wrongdoing, especially wronging a person.

To cover His bases, Jesus used both words here. He said debts in the prayer itself (twice in verse 12) and trespasses three times in His two-verse P.S. (verses 14 and 15). Jesus probably spoke this in Aramaic, which His Jewish contemporaries used as an oral substitute for Hebrew. But Matthew wrote in Greek, the universal language then and there, using *opheilema* for debts in verse 12 and *paraptoma* for trespasses in verses 14–15. So Jesus probably used different words as He mouthed this model prayer.

Why do we need to forgive the people who hurt us when the bottom falls out because someone betrayed us? The seven Scripture verses printed above have nine reasons we must plod past our pain to forgive those who hurt us or even betrayed us:

1) The Bible commands it.

2) Jesus said so.

3) God commands us to do it. So it's a new sin on us, if we disobey His command to forgive them.

4) Jesus instructs us to pray in this way.

5) It accomplishes our heavenly Father's will.

6) It is doing on earth what is done in heaven.

7) We are asking God to forgive us as we have forgiven those who wronged us.

8) Jesus promises that if we forgive others who have wronged us, God will forgive us.

9) Jesus warns us that if we don't forgive others, God will not forgive us.

These seven verses are not the only ones telling us to forgive those who hurt us. The instruction to forgive is all through the gospels and the New Testament. If you are having a hard time forgiving your betrayer, or others who hurt you, try reading these other passages daily until your bitterness passes and you can forgive them. Verses like these finally got through to one Christian woman who had a hard time forgiving because she had been hurt so badly. She finally got to the place where she could start praying, "Lord, I am not willing to forgive. But I'm willing for You to make me willing to forgive." See if these words from God's Word make you willing to forgive, or at least willing to be made willing.

Luke 11:4 links our "getting forgiveness" to "having given it." Luke 6:37 says, "Forgive, and you will be forgiven." Luke 23:34 has Jesus on the cross, praying for forgiveness for those crucifying Him. Like Peter, we may struggle to forgive our repeat offenders: "Lord, how often will my brother sin against me, and I forgive him? As many as seven times?" Jesus said to him, "I do not say to you seven times, but seventy-seven times" (Matthew 18:21–22). Read the story Jesus told Peter about how people who have been forgiven should be willing to forgive others (Matthew 18:23–35). The last verse was Jesus' punch line: "So also my heavenly Father will do to every one of you, if you do not forgive your brother from your heart."

Mark 11:25 echoes Christ's warning at the end of the Lord's Prayer: "And whenever you stand praying, forgive, if you have anything against anyone, so that your Father also who is in heaven may forgive you your trespasses." Some Bible translations add verse 26: "But if you do not forgive, neither will your Father who is in heaven forgive your sins."

Paul writes in Ephesians 4:32, "Be kind to one another, tender-hearted, forgiving one another, as God in Christ forgave you." Colossians 3:12 cites five attitudes that are prerequisites to forgiving others: compassion, kindness, humility, meekness, and patience. These lead to "bearing with one another and, if one has a complaint against another, forgiving each other; as the Lord has forgiven you, so you also must forgive" (Colossians 3:13).

Beating Bitterness

Unforgiveness can be accompanied by bitterness. Hebrews 12:14–15 packs practical relational insights into two verses: "Strive for peace with everyone, and for the holiness without which no one will see the Lord. See to it that no one fails to obtain the grace of God; that no 'root of bitterness' springs up and causes trouble, and by it many become defiled." Nip it in the bud, before it roots to trouble you or others.

Ephesians 4:29–32 implies that our bitterness grieves the Holy Spirit and commands us to forgive others because Christ paid the price for God to forgive us:

> Let no corrupting talk come out of your mouths, but only such as is good for building up, as fits the occasion, that it may give grace to those who hear. And do not grieve the Holy Spirit of God, by whom you were sealed for the day of redemption. Let all bitterness and wrath and anger and clamor and slander be put away from you, along with all malice. Be kind to one another, tenderhearted, forgiving one another, as God in Christ forgave you.

Follow the example in this testimony from a woman who beat bitterness and unforgiveness:

> When I had been wronged, God led me to the story in 2 Kings 6:15–23. I certainly didn't wish harm on my enemies. So, I carried a loaf of homemade bread and offered forgiveness face-to-face and an apology for any perceived wrongs that I had committed. Afterward, I began praying God's blessings for my offenders using Numbers 6:24–26, inserting their names in place of 'you.' The result has been a lifting of the bitterness in my heart."

The LORD bless you and keep you;
the LORD make his face to shine upon you and be gracious to you;
the LORD lift up his countenance upon you and give you peace
(Numbers 6:24–26).

CHAPTER 5

AARON, ALSO

Then the anger of the LORD was kindled against Moses and he said, "Is there not Aaron, your brother, the Levite? I know that he can speak well. Behold, he is coming out to meet you, and when he sees you, he will be glad in his heart. You shall speak to him and put the words in his mouth, and I will be with your mouth and with his mouth and will teach you both what to do. He shall speak for you to the people, and he shall be your mouth, and you shall be as God to him" (Exodus 4:14–16).

Moses and his only brother, Aaron, were three years apart at birth. They were just days apart in their deaths. But for the twelve decades they shared, they were worlds apart in their life situation and spiritual inclination. Exodus 4:14 is the first of 349 times Scripture mentions Aaron. Aaron was not exceptional as a person once we look past his position as Israel's first-ever high priest.

Let's start with the good. There are some Aaron assets in the above passage. First, he was a Levite, a respectable reference in the Bible books about that era. Second, he was the only brother of one of the two greatest leaders and most important characters in the whole Old Testament. Third, God complimented Aaron, saying he was a good speaker. Fourth, he has a sense of family loyalty. Moses had been gone for forty years. Not forgetting him, Aaron walked a long way seeking him. Finding the long-missed Moses brought Aaron heartfelt gladness. Fifth, Aaron was available and willing to be used in God's plans and purposes. Finally, he was religious and willing for his little brother to be as God to him.

This sixth strength is a hinge, which swings the door back in the other direction. If Moses was as God to Aaron, then God was not as God to Aaron. Aaron typifies millions through the millennia who may have known God personally but whose relationship with Him was mainly indirect and second-hand. They relate to God primarily through someone who knows God better and has a closer relationship.

For many church members this person is their pastor. It could be their Sunday school teacher, small group leader, friend, or relative. Many testimonies cast a godly grandmother in this role.

This second-hand spirituality haunts Aaron as we trace his story. It will hamstring the fledgling Hebrew nation at a crucial point in their development. Aaron never had a burning-bush encounter with God or a solo date with the deity as Moses did. So, this was second-hand to him, if and when Moses told him about it. His default strategy was experiencing God through Moses, until a year after the exodus from Egypt. He finally saw God on a group plan with about eighty other people one evening (Exodus 24:1–2, 9–11).

Twelve Years a Slave is an 1853 memoir and slave narrative of Solomon Northup, an African American man who was born free in upstate New York. On a trip to Washington, D. C., in the prime of life, he was kidnapped and sold into slavery in the South. He endured a harsh master in Louisiana, but after a dozen years, he escaped back to the free North. In defense of Aaron, he was a slave seven times that long in Egypt and was an old man when finally tapped for his leadership role.

"Follow the money" is a common trail in criminal investigations. In the Exodus 4:14–16 passage above, a follow-the-message trail is evident. Trace how the Lord's message gets to Aaron. It starts with God and then travels to Moses (maybe his ears first but then to his mind). The next stop is Moses' mouth, which sends it straight to Aaron's mouth. Like mouth-to mouth resuscitation, this was mouth-to-mouth recitation.

Taking the text literally, it was not God but Moses for whom Aaron spoke, whose mouth he was. It was Moses who "put the words in his mouth." Conspicuous by its absence is any reference to Aaron's thought process in the transfer. He parroted what Moses passed on to him. Hopefully, he pondered it afterward. There may have been mental memory, but it did not stick spiritually. He did not hide God's word in his heart or meditate on it.

The Bible usually mentions Aaron with someone else and rarely by himself. Aaron is the Bible's "Mister Also." The phrase "Aaron also" occurs in Exodus 29:44 ESV and elsewhere in other translations. The obvious other is Moses. "Moses and Aaron" occurs sixty-nine times in the Bible. These verses verify him as Moses' secondhand shadow. The only four reverse-order cases of "Aaron and Moses" are genealogical, and this was because he was born first.

Psalm 103:7 is a Moses verse where Aaron's absence is striking: "He (the Lord) made known his ways unto Moses, his acts unto the children of Israel" (KJV). Aaron did not know God's ways for himself. When he was apart from Moses, Aaron had no inner compass pointing him to God's true north.

There are a few references to Aaron and "her" (his sister, Miriam), without mention of their brother, Moses. A man named Hur partnered with Aaron at a crisis time. Aaron's best instrument was second fiddle. Hur and Aaron are legitimate nominees for the Bible's best-supporting actor, for their mountaintop performance in Israel's first skirmish in the wilderness:

So Joshua did as Moses said to him, and fought with Amalek.
And Moses, Aaron, and Hur went up to the top of the hill. And so

it was, when Moses held up his hand, that Israel prevailed; and when he let down his hand, Amalek prevailed. But Moses' hands became heavy; so they took a stone and put it under him, and he sat on it. And Aaron and Hur supported his hands, one on one side, and the other on the other side; and his hands were steady until the going down of the sun. So Joshua defeated Amalek and his people with the edge of the sword (Exodus 17: 10–13, NKJV).

Aaron was also an "also" with his sons since they were the priests under him and with him. Scripture cites this group over one hundred times. Aaron was the subject — he was grouped with his sons on fifty-six occasions. In fifty-three instances, his sons were the subject but referenced with their father. There are over twenty more references to "son(s) of Aaron" or "children of Aaron."

Most Bible verses that name just Aaron concern his priestly position. They describe how he was purified for this, what he put on to do that, and what various things he did as he performed this role. As with leaders today in church or government, we respect the position of leadership, even as we recognize flaws of the person in leadership. We should respect Aaron's role as a high priest as he performed the sacrifices that temporarily restored the Hebrews' fellowship with their covenant God. We especially reverence him as the type and shadow of our Great High Priest, the Lord Jesus (Hebrews 4:14–5:10).

It is interesting to speculate whether Moses' brother would have had a cameo role had Moses had the faith to answer God's call immediately and unconditionally, instead of continuing to protest because of his perceived faults and limitations. The Lord was patient through the first four of Moses' misgivings (Exodus 3:11, 13; 4:1, 10). God spent twenty-one verses of explanation answering these four verses of Moses' excuses. The fourth explanation adds a quick display of four miracles through Moses.

When four explanations and demonstrations failed to convince Moses, God ran out of patience with Moses' lack of faith. God's Plan A was Moses flying solo. But when Moses pleads the fifth excuse, "O my Lord, please send by the hand of whomever else You may send," God gets mad and pulls the trigger for Plan B:

> *Then the anger of the* LORD *was kindled against Moses and he said, "Is there not Aaron, your brother, the Levite? I know that he can speak well. Behold, he is coming out to meet you … . He shall speak for you … and he shall be your mouth'" (Exodus 4:14, 16).*

Lest we too quickly pile blame on Moses for this misstep, we should realize that whenever we point a finger at someone, we have three fingers pointing back at ourselves. How many times over the course of our lives have we settled for second or third-best instead of taking an initial but immediate step of faith into God's perfect will for that moment? We have plenty of company in Scripture. Ishmael was Abraham's Plan B as he got impatient waiting for Isaac. Jacob was Rebekah's Plan B for the father's blessing Isaac intended for Esau. Rachel's maid Bilhah was her Plan B for making babies for Jacob before God gave Joseph and Benjamin to Rachel.

The Moses we know in retrospect is supersized spiritually from Midian's mumbler we meet in Exodus chapters 2–4. The only prior introduction Moses had to Yahweh, or indoctrination in His ways, was as he was weaned by his mother Jochebed. Next followed almost four decades of learning about the many Egyptian gods and another four decades in Midian.

Moses' father-in-law, Jethro, is thrice called "priest of Midian" (Exodus 2:16; 3:1; 18:1). The Midianites were monotheistic, but by the time the teaching of the God of Abraham had rippled all the way to them, it had been watered down and warped. Midianite traders were traitors to Joseph, selling him to the Ishmaelites, who trafficked him into Egyptian slavery. Although Moses' true Hebrew identity had surfaced in his last days in the palace, his bold but brash attempt to act on it had backfired into an abysmal failure.

We're taking advantage of 20/20 hindsight on Moses. He spoke up on his own without Aaron on numerous appearances before Pharaoh, the world's most powerful ruler. In fact, Moses did all the talking before Pharaoh in the ten times of announcement and pronouncement of the ten plagues. Aaron was the speaker on the first occasion after he and Moses crossed the border back into Egypt (Exodus 4:30). But this was just Goshen, as they shared the plan with their Hebrew kin.

The Hebrews in Egypt had not seen Moses for forty years but had lived with Aaron for eight decades. Aaron was more comfortable and confident with this group, speaking in their shared heart language to the people he had lived with for eighty-three years. His speaking and "his signs in the sight of the people" served the purpose this time: "And the people believed; and when they heard that the Lord had visited the people of Israel and that he had seen their affliction, they bowed their heads and worshiped" (Exodus 4:31).

The Bible's next verse (Exodus 5:1) has Moses and Aaron telling Pharaoh, "Thus says the Lord, the God of Israel: 'Let My people go, that they may hold a feast to Me in the wilderness.'" The wording does not nail down the speaker(s). Was it Moses or Aaron? Or did they both get in on the action? Verse 3 has the same ambiguity: "So they said." The situation grew worse, not better. Instead of releasing the Hebrews, Pharaoh tightened his grip. He made the taskmasters stop providing the straw the slaves used in making bricks without reducing their quota of bricks (Exodus 5: 6–13). And the Hebrews who had worked their way up to stewards were beaten (5:14) to underscore the point. Understandably, the stewards confronted Moses and Aaron about this, blaming them for the offense and its punishment (5:20–21).

The following ten verses are a dialogue between Moses and God with no mention of Aaron (Exodus 5:22–6:8). Then Moses spoke to the children of Israel, "but they did not listen to Moses, because of their broken spirit and harsh slavery" (6:9). A three-verse argument between Moses and the Lord (6:10–12) concludes with the Lord's one-verse reminder to Moses and Aaron of their original mission to Pharaoh, which God had not withdrawn or watered down (6:13).

Next follows what seems to be a dozen verses of diversion (Exodus 6:14–27). It is a genealogy of Levi's branch of the patriarch Jacob's family tree from Levi through his three sons, mainly Kohath. The focus is two of Kohath's four sons: Amram and Izhar.

Amram fathered Moses and Aaron. Aaron's four sons are listed, with the attention on his two descendants who would follow him as Israel's high priests: Aaron's son Eleazer and grandson Phinehas.

Izhar's three sons are listed with the focus on Korah's three sons. The sons of Korah were historical people, but Exodus 6:24 and 1 Chronicles 6:22–23 are the only Bible verses that supply all three names: Assir, Elkanah, and Abiasaph.

When the action resumes and God's message must move on to Pharaoh, Moses reverts to his mumbler mantra:

But Moses said to the LORD, "Behold, I am of uncircumcised lips. How will Pharaoh listen to me?" And the LORD said to Moses, "See, I have made you like God to Pharaoh, and your brother Aaron shall be your prophet. You shall speak all that I command you, and your brother Aaron shall tell Pharaoh ..." (Exodus 6:30–7:2).

But the ensuing chapters never quote anything Aaron said to Pharaoh. There are some reports of their interactions with Pharaoh.

"Now Moses was eighty years old, and Aaron eighty-three years old, when they spoke to Pharaoh" (Exodus 7:7). "Moses and Aaron went in to Pharaoh and said ..." (10:3). There are some reports of his response to them: "He would not listen to them ..." (7:13, 22; 8:15; 9:12). Aaron's inclusion was God's permissive will but not His perfect will, so sacred Scripture never records even a word which Aaron spoke solo to Pharaoh.

Bottomed Out

Have you ever been hurt by someone who was supposed to be helping you? Most of us have. Its seriousness and severity impacted the wound's depth and duration, and whether it left a scar. I've been on the giving end of the wound with my only brother. Dad never had many tools, but one he did have was a garden tool called a mattock. Steve was often my best playmate, but one day I got mad at him and hit him in the mouth with the mattock. It drew blood, and one parent carried him for medical treatment. I can't see a scar on his face now, but it is probably still in his memory bank.

My other low point came after Mom received a new dining room suite. Boys back then loved to make airplanes out of three board scraps. The longest was the fuselage, the next longest was the wing, and the shortest was the tail. You laid the longest one flat on your workbench, placed the other two on top of it, and nailed them. Dad had no bench, so we used Mom's new table, but our nails were too long. When I went to pick up our plane, it would not "take off." Being the first to realize this, I said, "Steve, look what you've done!" I was shocked that we were not spanked, but when Mom came home from work, she blamed it on our housekeeper for letting preschoolers use the dining room as a workshop. Who has left scars on your body, in your memory, or on your psyche?

Battling Back

Time heals many wounds, but only God can heal the rest. Don't try to conjure bad memories, just deal with the ones that still bother you. Give them to God, take your hands off them, and ask Him to them away.

You have probably not been wronged to the degree that Aaron and Moses' great uncle Joseph was. Reread his story in Genesis 37:12–36, chapters 39–45, and 50:15–21. It may take you several days to do this, but don't rush. It will be more realistic if you quit for the day whenever there is a new day in the story.

Reread those last seven verses seven times.

Then memorize one verse: Genesis 50:20. Repeat it several times a day until you have it down. Once you do, ask the Lord to make this verse true for you as He did for Joseph.

Next read Romans 8:26–30 for several days and grasp its meaning.

Then memorize Romans 8:28–29, saying it several times a day. Most people memorize just verse 28, but verse 29 is how God works verse 28.

Finally, make a list of your painful memories that remain. Pray and claim Romans 8:28–29 for each of these. As a ministry, ask God to lead you to those who may be blessed and helped by your accounts of how God has helped turn your bitterness into forgiveness.

CHAPTER 6

REUBEN, REUBEN:
DATHAN AND ABIRAM

Now Korah ... and Dathan and Abiram ... and On ... sons of Reuben, took men. And they rose up before Moses (Numbers 16:1–2).

The American Film Institute lists *Hotel Rwanda* as one of the one hundred most inspirational movies of all time. This 2004 film was critically acclaimed and nominated for multiple Academy awards. It told the 1994 story of the Rwandan genocide. The Rwandan genocide saw an estimated 500,000 to one million Rwandans killed in a one hundred-day period. This genocide killed a fifth of Rwanda's population, but the conflict was between just two of its tribes, the Hutu and the Tutsi.

Our true story, which the New Testament calls Korah's rebellion (Jude 11), was actually a conflict between two of Israel's twelve tribes, Levi and Reuben. And as the Hutu majority government killed moderate Hutu, along with their mass slaughter of Tutsi, so the core of Korah's conflict was between families within the tribe of Levi. But Korah hawked this plot to kindred spirit Reubenites, and they jumped on the bandwagon. There is no question that the whole thing was Korah's idea. He was the instigator who took the initiative. But before he went to Moses the leader, he went to Reuben the loser.

Why did Korah go to the sons of Reuben when sowing the seeds of his rebellion? It began with convenience and constant contact. The two million Israelites were camped on the four sides of the tabernacle with three tribes on each side. On the south side (Numbers 2:10–16) were Reuben, Simeon, and Gad. Moses and Aaron camped east, just outside the only entrance into the tabernacle courtyard. The rest of the tribe of Levi camped in the other three directions, based on Levi's three sons: Gerson, Kohath, and Merari.

Korah was among the Kohathites, camped on the south side. The south side was called "the camp of Reuben" (Numbers 2:16), and this tribe led this quadrant when they marched. The Kohathites pitched closest to the tabernacle's southern exterior, followed by Reuben, Simeon, and Gad. So, the Kohathites and Reubenites were next-door neighbors.

Reubenites passed by or through the Kohathite tents to gather with the congregation or go to the tabernacle. Whenever the Kohathites ventured out into the south side, they had to start with or go through the Reubenite section. We must be careful with whom we associate because we can be influenced by them.

Because the Levites' work included the physical labor of carrying the tabernacle and its components (plus taking it apart and putting it back together every time they moved), their active service was from age thirty to fifty (Numbers 4:3, 23, 30). Because their fathers were brothers (Numbers 6:18–21), Korah was contemporary in age with Aaron and Moses.

Since Moses was eighty when God sent him back to Egypt to deliver the Hebrews, Korah was past mandatory retirement age for Levites. Besides an idle mind being the devil's workshop, which seemed to happen with Korah, his lack of specific responsibilities may have relegated him to the rear of the Levites' camp. This would have located him at the Levite/Reubenite boundary line. Korah had back-row rank and responsibility but wanted front-row credit and control. He found this with the two Reubenites whose tents pitched just behind his: Dathan and Abiram.

These two recruited their tribesman, On. He was hesitant until they promised him that Moses and Aaron would resign without resistance once they saw the multitude and magnitude of the opposition. On strolled beside the three ringleaders as they approached the showdown. But as they lined up against Moses and Aaron, On followed a hunch to step back into the crowd. His absence from the story's continuation in Numbers 16:12–15, 24–27 implies he had a change of heart and withdrew from the opposition. Once Moses argued back against Korah's opening salvo, On could see this coup would not be bloodless.

As the 250 rebels faced forward, On kept moving backward. Once he reached their back row, he kept walking backward. He turned and ran back to his tent, content to learn later how things went. On was precursor to a Reubenite trait, the paralysis of indecision, that surfaced during the judgeship of Deborah and the battles of Barak. In *The Message*, Eugene Peterson phrases it this way: "But in Reuben's divisions was much second-guessing. Why all those campfire discussions? Diverted and distracted, Reuben's divisions couldn't make up their minds" (Judges 5:15–16). The word "repent" means "to change one's mind." On changed his mind just in time, and got out while the getting was good.

Besides geographical proximity, Levites and Reubenites were more blood-related with a stronger kinship tie. The sons of Jacob had four mothers. Levi and Reuben had the same one, Jacob's first wife, Leah.

In the southeastern U.S. are many churches dominated by one or more extended families. They can band together to oppose and prevent any changes that go against their church traditions or personal preferences. My friend Wendell Estep, a westerner, discovered this at his first church in the deep South. It stumped him for five years until an insight from his friend Morris Chapman, a southerner who moved to pastor in the West. Chapman explained that "in the South, the red runs deep. People will not cross a blood relationship to do the right thing in church. This deep red extends to marriage and business relationships, and even neighbors or co-workers."

The red ran deep in Leah's side of the family. When Korah began to hatch his plot, he found a sympathetic ear in Reubenite relatives on his mother's side of the family tree.

Reuben was easy pickings because of hurt feelings and tarnished pride. Reuben had become the most disenfranchised and had lost the most of Jacob's twelve sons. As Jacob's only firstborn, Reuben would have expected the double portion due the firstborn in that era. But the other tribes took the prize.

The kingship began in Benjamin with Saul. Starting with David, the royal realm switched permanently to Judah. Reuben saw his brother Levi get the religious realm from top to bottom. The religious workers were even called Levites. The Levi tribe were the religious leaders too, the priests and high priest. Not even the initial national leaders came from firstborn Reuben. Levi double-dipped with Moses as Israel's first overall leader. His successor Joshua was from the tribe of Ephraim. Reubenites felt right to resent.

Jacob understandably favored Rachel. He loved her and worked seven years to marry her until Laban pulled a bait-and-switch with Leah. God loved Leah, so He gave Jacob a reason to love her, too.

When the LORD saw that Leah was unloved, He opened her womb; but Rachel was barren. So Leah conceived and bore a son, and she called his name Reuben; for she said, "The LORD has surely looked on my affliction. Now therefore, my husband will love me" (Genesis 29:31–32, NKJV).

Having a baby did not solve marital strife then any more than it does now. Leah bore Jacob three more sons, including Levi, before Jacob sired eight more children through his two wives and their two maids.

The mothers passed their family squabbles to their sons. Rachel's first child was Joseph, whom his siblings would sell into slavery. He was taken to Egypt where he became famous. His hate-filled half-brothers had planned to kill Joseph, but Reuben intervened, selling them on the idea to sell him as a slave instead. Reuben actually planned to free Joseph before this happened, but the brothers expedited the sale while Reuben was gone.

Saving Joseph's life was Reuben's high-water mark. But he sank to loathsome lows when he "went and lay with Bilhah, his father's concubine" (Genesis 35:22). Sins don't stay secret, so Jacob heard about it. This was not just boys being boys — a case of teenage testosterone. It stoked the flames of conflict, as Bilhah was the maid of Rachel, Reuben's mother Leah's rival. It was also incest since Bilhah was the mother of Reuben's half-brothers, Dan and Naphtali — and dishonoring to Reuben's father, Jacob.

Jacob never forgot nor forgave this. On his deathbed in Egypt, he gathered his sons to tell their futures (Genesis 49:1–2). In chronological order, he started with Reuben and started positive: "Reuben, you are my firstborn, my might, and the firstfruits of my strength, preeminent in dignity and preeminent in power" (49:3).

Reuben's smile is short-lived, as the last half of Jacob's prophecy recalls how the incest infected him and infuriated his dad: "Unstable as water, you shall not have preeminence, because you went up to your father's bed; then you defiled it — he went up to my couch!" (49:4). Reuben inherited the excellence of the firstborn, but, like his uncle Esau, he pawned permanent honor to satisfy passing passions.

Even before Reuben's tragic mistake, his firstborn status was not leveraged into actions worth scriptural note. A group rarely surpasses its leader, so the Reubenites continued to content themselves with the commonplace. The one Reubenite who had a golden opportunity to reverse the pattern was Shammua. At the time of the twelve spies, he was the Reubenite identified as "a chief among them" (Numbers 13:1–4). He is named first of the spies, so Reuben was still functioning as the firstborn tribe.

In this role, Shammua had the leadership and leverage to have made the motion on behalf of the spies for the Israelites to enter the Promised Land immediately. In group discussions in general, and particularly in official ones where decisions are made on actions to be taken, the opening comment sets the tone and direction of what follows. The spies brought back impressive samples of native fruits, and the introduction in the spies' report paved the way for Shammua to set the pace:

> *At the end of forty days they returned from spying out the land. And they came to Moses and Aaron and to all the congregation of the people of Israel … . They brought back word to them and to all the congregation, and showed them the fruit of the land. And they told him, "We came to the land to which you sent us. It flows with milk and honey, and this is its fruit" (Numbers 13:25–27).*

This preface confirmed details in God's first description of this land. At the burning bush, God told Moses that He would bring the people to "a land flowing with milk and honey" (Exodus 3:8). Once the spies saw the milk and honey, this was proof that anything and everything God had promised about Canaan was true. This confirmation would also have buoyed the congregation, preparing them to follow the spies back into this land God had promised them.

There was a pause at this point, obviously a transition. Representing the firstborn, it was in Shammua's prerogative to stand up, step up, and speak up. His genes bore the "beginning of strength and the excellency of dignity and power" which the patriarch Jacob had acknowledged. But Shammua failed to see or seize the *carpe diem* that stared him in the face. Instead of showing the lion boldness of the righteous (Proverbs 28:1), all he could manage was a deer in the headlights look. Had he simply made the motion to enter the Promised Land, Caleb would have seconded it (Numbers 13:30) and Joshua would have joined in (Numbers 14:6–9). Too bad Shammua did not know the hymn *On Jordan's Stormy Banks* and belt out its chorus: "I am bound for the promised land, I am bound for the promised land; O who will come and go with me? I am bound for the promised land."

Shammua's silence gave the naysayers the floor. Jesus warned later that he who tries to save his life will lose it, but one willing to lose his life for God's sake will save it (Mark 8:35). Shammua the Reubenite exemplified this. He is never named after this event and is not among the three Reubenite leaders recruited by Korah two chapters later. What happened to Shammua, who did not have the faith to make to motion to enter the promised land? Paul wrote, "Whatever does not proceed from faith is sin" (Romans 14:23), and "the wages of sin is death" (Romans 6:23).

And the men whom Moses sent to spy out the land, who returned and made all the congregation grumble against him by bringing a bad report about the land ... died by plague before the LORD *(Numbers 14:36–37).*

A later incident echoed the Reubenites' shortsightedness, fickleness, and vulnerability to schemes. They would settle for less than the best, opting for pretty pastureland on the wrong side of the Jordan, instead of a parcel within the land promised by God (Deuteronomy 3:12–17;

Joshua 13:15–23).

The Reubenite men met Joshua's demand that they cross the Jordan River to help their brother tribes conquer the Promised Land (Joshua 1:12–15; 4:12), but they left their wives and children outside the Promised Land. After meeting their military commitments, they crossed the Jordan back to their families in the unpromised land. They settled for less than God's full protection and blessings. The distance would make it harder to make the three annual pilgrimages to the tabernacle or temple for the feasts of Israel. Living among other nations would later contribute to their being among the first Israelite tribes to lose their territories to pagan peoples.

The Reubenites talked a better game than they played. When Joshua reminded them they had promised Moses to send their soldiers to help conquer Canaan, they piously replied, "All that you have commanded us we will do, and wherever you send us we will go. Just as we obeyed Moses in all things, so we will obey you" (Joshua 1:16–17). How quickly they had forgotten that three of the four leaders named in Korah's revolt against Moses' authority had come from their tribe. The verse after they were named with Korah shows how God saw their attitudes and actions: "Korah ... and certain Reubenites ... became insolent and rose up against Moses" (Numbers 16:1–2, NIV).

When the heat was on, the Reubenites tended to melt. When Moses did not wilt before Korah but stood up to him, the Reubenites slipped back to their tents. When summoned back by Moses to take responsibility for their actions, they lacked the courage to come, using revisionist history for their excuse:

> And Moses sent to call Dathan and Abiram ... and they said, "We will not come up. Is it a small thing that you have brought us up out of a land flowing with milk and honey, to kill us in

the wilderness, that you must also make yourself a prince over us? Moreover, you have not brought us into a land flowing with milk and honey, nor given us inheritance of fields and vineyards. Will you put out the eyes of these men? We will not come up" (Numbers 16:12–14).

Dathan and Abiram refused to return to Moses or to show up for the showdown at sunup. But the showdown at sunup would make house calls.

Benched

Reuben was benched as the firstborn for lack of leadership and example. When the bottom falls out on us, there can be ripple effects. Collateral damage! Our immediate focus is the incident itself: when the bottom fell out. As the dust settles and our initial shock subsides, we begin to realize the earthquake that jolted us brings aftershocks.

A minor injury in my thirties taught me this. Nancy and I were invited for tennis at the home of rich friends. Our thrill ended abruptly when I fell on their court with a sprained right ankle, the first domino. My doctor treated me the next morning, and the pain was minor after that. The second domino was two weeks on crutches, which benched my driving. Each time another activity was benched, it caught me off guard. I could not even pour myself a cup of coffee and sit to enjoy it. Using my crutches took both hands, leaving me helpless to carry a cup of hot coffee to the nearest chair. These inconveniences were not traumatic, but they taught me to be thankful when my whole body works.

Bottomed Out

My last day as a sixty-eight-year-old was the continental divide in my adult medical history. I've had more injuries and surgeries since that day, than in the forty-seven years before. Playing the net in doubles tennis, I tore the medial meniscus in my right knee. My surgery went well. Rehab was short and almost painless. But three things got benched: participating in doubles with my wife, doing one of my favorite cardio exercises, and playing tennis for about twenty months — since I was afraid to get back on the court.

As you do a quick inventory of the times the bottom fell out on you, or on friends, relatives, neighbors or coworkers, what are some ways these people also got benched? The worse the bottom falls out, the more likely for benching in its wake. It can be a domino effect. For example, a seemingly healthy spouse gets a terminal diagnosis, which becomes ground zero for the bottom falling out on the family. Everything gets benched for this patient, especially if the malfunction is irreversible — the cancer has metastasized or the disease has advanced. The spouse and children are in the wake and feel the blow of each round of bad news.

The bottom will fall out first on our emotions. We may be flooded with a gamut of negative feelings: shock, hurt, fear, anger, disappointment, worry, pressure, disbelief, etc. Denying such feelings is counterproductive, so own them and process them.

Some emotions will dissipate on their own, but other feelings will persist and grow. Our feelings get out of control, like teenage hormones, so we are tempted to bench them and plod zombie-like through this ordeal.

But the Psalms encourage us to tell God our feelings, even the angry ones. Read Psalms 88 and 42 to see how the sons of Korah did this. David was even more vitriolic in Psalm 38, and the Bible calls him "a man after God's own heart" in both Testaments (1 Samuel 13:14; Acts 13:22). Psalm 34:18 promises, "The LORD is near to the brokenhearted and saves the crushed in spirit." So let God know you are and invite Him into this.

The bottom may continue to fall out in the medical area. Since medicine is not an exact science and the human body is so complex, the initial diagnosis may be more general with various diagnostics done days on end. Our patience, calm, courtesy, and positive attitude get benched. We will look back on this in embarrassed amazement, but the medical profession sees this daily, and understands this as par for the course. Patients lose patience, as do their families. Anger is not a sin; it is an emotion. But festering anger makes us more likely to sin. God made the human psyche to handle one day's worth of anger. Its interest compounds daily after that! "Be angry and do not sin; do not let the sun go down on your anger, and give no opportunity to the devil" (Ephesians 4:26–27).

A prolonged health crisis can bench our finances. It may drain our savings, liquidate investments, cancel vacation plans, or do even worse. Expenses soar, even with health insurance. A negative prognosis may cost the job of one breadwinner and cut the hours and pay of the other income earner. Let all your creditors know when extenuating circum-stances put your obligations above your resources. Some of them may have ways to write off or reduce some of your debts.

If the bottom falls out because of a sudden death or fatal accident, most of the above scenarios will be compacted and concentrated. If another person is involved, matters get even more convoluted and complicated. Expand the number of your prayer partners and the frequency of your updates to them.

Battling Back

Jesus promised His disciples that the Holy Spirit would "teach us all things" (John 14:26) and "guide us into all the truth" (John 16:13). He can use things from the natural world to illustrate spiritual principles. "But it is not the spiritual that is first but the natural, and then the spiritual" (1 Corinthians 15:46). The Spirit gave me some life applications from what I learned about the menisci that our Creator put in our knees.

> "The menisci protect the lower part of the leg from the shock of our body weight. Two wedge-shaped pieces of fibrocartilage act as shock absorbers between your femur and tibia. They help to transmit weight from one bone to the other and play an important role in knee stability. The outer portion of the meniscus, often referred to as the 'red zone,' has a good blood supply and can sometimes heal on its own if the tear is small. In contrast, the inner two-thirds of the meniscus, known as the 'white zone,' does not have a good blood supply. Tears in this portion will not heal on their own, as this area lacks blood vessels to bring in healing nutrients."
> *(Excerpted from orthoinfo.aaos.org)*

This brief explanation twice mentions weight. As you battle back from the bottom falling out on you, is there any excess weight (physically or figuratively) in your life that you should shed, to become more fit for the battles of life? Hebrews 12:1 ends with, "Let us also lay aside every weight, and sin which clings so closely, and let us run with endurance the race that is set before us." One or two issues may come to your mind, but prayerfully ask the Lord to reveal anything else that He sees weighing you down. Put a marker in your Bible at Psalm 139:23–24 for a good way to word this to God: "Search me, O God, and know my heart! Try me and know my thoughts! And see if there be any grievous way in me, and lead me in the way everlasting!"

If you need extra motivation or encouragement to do this, pair the first half of Hebrews 12:1 with its last half quoted in the above paragraph: "Therefore, since we are surrounded by so great a cloud of witnesses … ."

This cloud of witnesses refers to all the Old Testament characters named or grouped in the eleventh chapter and extends through New Testament saints to people the last two thousand years who have preceded us to heaven and can view us from there. Think of your loved ones who have gone to be with the Lord, who are looking down on you with interest. Was there a Sunday school teacher who shaped your life, led you to Christ, or discipled you? Was there a pastor who fed you with God's Word? One preacher called this cloud of witnesses our "balcony people," cheering you on as you fight the battles of life. A mental picture of them may spur you on as you battle back from the bottom falling out on you, and as you press on to get in shape spiritually.

Early on, the Bible reveals that blood is life, and life is in the blood (Genesis 9:4; Exodus 17:11, 14; Deuteronomy 12:23). Our physical life confirms this at the macro and micro levels. If too much blood flows out of your body, you die. But the tiny sample of your blood drawn at the lab can help save your life by revealing so much on your body's components and functions. When you have a wound or injury, your body tries to send blood there to help heal it. When the bottom falls out on us, we must think and act like a red zone meniscus and let the help and healing flow into our hurts and hardships.

As you battle back from the bottom falling out on you, your goal line may feel ninety-nine yards away. But where there is life, there is hope. When there is still time, there is hope. And when God is on our team, we have a chance. Be like the lateral meniscus, a red zone with a blood supply, which can bring hope and healing.

Backstory

The three main characters in this chapter's Backstory had all been benched in various ways. Their main response was to grumble about it.

Now these things took place as examples for us, that we might not desire evil as they did ... nor grumble, as some of them did and were destroyed by the Destroyer. Now these things happened to them as an example, but they were written down for our instruction, on whom the end of the ages has come. Therefore let anyone who thinks that he stands take heed lest he fall. No temptation has overtaken you that is not common to man. God is faithful, and he will not let you be tempted beyond your ability, but with the temptation he will also provide the way of escape, that you may be able to endure it (1 Corinthians 10:6, 10–13).

CHAPTER 7

AARON, SOLO

On the rare occasions when the Bible quotes Aaron solo, he blows it. Forty is Scripture's symbolic number for testing, and Aaron flunked his first big test. Exodus 24:18–32:14 records Moses' first forty-day visit with God on top of Mount Sinai to receive the tabernacle specs and the tablets of stone etched with the Ten Commandments.

Moses let the elders know that Aaron and Hur were in charge during his absence:

So Moses rose with his assistant Joshua, and Moses went up into the mountain of God. And he said to the elders, "Wait here for us until we return to you. And behold, Aaron and Hur are with you. Whoever has a dispute, let him go to them" (Exodus 24:13–14).

What Happened to Hur?

The key passage above names a quartet of Israel's leaders, ending with Hur. He is best known for helping Joshua hold up Moses' hands in Exodus 17:8–13, the secret weapon in Israel's defeat of Amalek. Most Bible readers fail to notice his absence when the dispute anticipated above happens eight chapters later in Exodus 32:1–6. It is unthinkable that Hur would have stood by silently while Joshua's caving to the crowd cost three thousand lives, or that Joshua would not have stalled the crowd while sending for Hur. What happened to Hur?

There are some clues which shed light. "Jewish tradition is that he was the husband of Miriam" ("Hur," Young's Analytical Concordance). If so, this must have been a late-life union, as the Bible never mentions a spouse or children for Miriam. By contrast, it says five times that Hur's son, Uri, was the father of Bezaleel, the master craftsman of the tabernacle (Exodus 31:2; 36:30; 38:22; 1 Chronicles 2:20; 2 Chronicles 1:5). The key factor may be just two chapters before Korah's rebellion when God says in Numbers 14:28–30 that everyone over age twenty, except Caleb and Joshua, will die in the wilderness before Israel enters Canaan (Numbers 14:28–30).

The natural deaths of almost two million people may have begun immediately. This may have followed a general pattern of oldest to youngest. Miriam, Moses and Aaron were octogenarians when they heard their death sentence. Miriam and Aaron will die before the end of Numbers and Moses before the end of the Bible's next book, Deuteronomy.

This writer believes Hur may have been among the oldest Hebrews in the exodus from Egypt. The Bible cites Hur's genealogy four times after the golden calf episode, but Hur never appears in the biblical narrative after Moses said he and Aaron would hold the fort while Moses was away with God. The writer also believes the most plausible reason Hur was not at Aaron's side to ask the people to wait one more day for Moses is that he died of natural causes in the forty-day period Moses was away on the mount.

What Happened to Aaron?

Near the end of the forty days, the people become tired of waiting for Moses. They wanted to walk by sight instead of by faith. They crowded around Aaron, almost suffocating him. They kept pressuring him to make them a god they could see (Exodus 32:1). He kept putting them off, hoping that Moses would finally show up to take charge again and restore order.

American Christians stand on the shoulders of billions of Christ-followers around the globe who for two millennia have stood firm in their faith in a God we can't see. Thousands of our brothers and sisters have been willing to make the ultimate sacrifice, surrendering their life, rather than capitulate to a god worshipped in the form of some physical manifestation.

Wherever they and their spiritual forbears have been for centuries, they have been surrounded and often ruled by peoples who can show them their god(s) or at least the idols that represent them. In Canaan, it was just one main male God, Baal, and a female deity with her Asherah poles (mentioned thirty times in the Bible). For four centuries, they had seen the hundreds of Egyptian gods, who kept them in bondage until their invisible God finally sent some plagues to set them free. He had promised them the land of Canaan. But one year later, they were still stuck in the desert with nothing to eat but manna and often no water nearby.

This was Aaron's golden opportunity to stand up and speak up for God. He could have reminded them that Moses had promised to return from his mountaintop experience with God. He could have recounted how the Lord had made good on every promise and met the Hebrews' every need. He could have stressed that their invisible God had been invincible in exposing and expunging the visible Egyptian gods.

But the Bible does not imply that Aaron offered any resistance or tried to talk them out of it. As "Aaron Also," he was a thermometer, not a thermostat. If he had asked them to merely think and pray about it overnight, before they pulled the trigger on such a monumental shift, Moses would have been back.

At this pivotal point, Aaron tripped up in sin's trifecta. He sinned by commission, omission, and disposition. He failed to display an attitude of faith and did not speak up for the one true God. He even stooped to concoct the plan for and craft with his own hands their divergent deity

(Exodus 32:2–4). He tried to legitimize it by counterfeiting a festival to the Lord. A shaky festival to a shady god soured quickly, and idolatry erupted into immorality (32:5–6). Aaron's sin here was not just a slip of the tongue. He had the gall to state twice this satanic sacrilege, "These are your gods, O Israel, who brought you up out of Egypt!" (32:4).

One characteristic of a good leader is willingness to admit mistakes and take the blame for his responsibility. When Moses showed up that evening, to do disaster relief, Aaron wanted to pass the buck. "Moses said to Aaron, 'What did this people do to you that you have brought such a great sin upon them?' And Aaron said, 'Let not the anger of my lord burn hot'" (Exodus 32:21–22).

Note that Hur is not mentioned in Moses' rebuke as he starts down the chain of command for the pro-tem leadership. Moses may have started but stopped with his brother who had the ongoing authority as High Priest, while Hur was "just a layman."

There are six more possibilities. First, as suggested seven paragraphs above, Hur may have died in the forty-day period between being named by Moses as a co-leader in his absence and the occasion to exercise this authority. Second, Moses may have seen Aaron first, scolded him, and then went to find Hur. Third, Hur may have been absent at the moment because he tried to stand up against the people, but Aaron rejected his counsel and sent him away. Fourth, Hur may have stood up against the rebels, who rejected his warning and removed him from the scene. Fifth, since the rebellion ignited quickly, Hur may have been absent for whatever reason and, thus, unavailable to bolster Aaron's resistance of the rebels. Sixth, Hur may have capitulated to the rebels and died in God's judgment of them. Since Hur disappears from the Bible's narrative after Exodus 24, all explanations for his escaping any mention of blame in the golden calf judgment are merely interpretations.

Recall that Moses was "like God" to Aaron. When Moses was away with God, it seemed to Aaron that God was absent, too. "You know how prone these people are to evil. They said to me, 'Make us gods who will go before us' … . Then they gave me the gold, and I threw it into the fire, and out came this calf!" (Exodus 32:21–24, NIV).

The gold was actually Aaron's idea. And he became the goldsmith.

> So Aaron said to them, "Take off the rings of gold that are in the ears of your wives, your sons, and your daughters, and bring them to me." … And he received the gold from their hand and fashioned it with a graving tool and made a golden calf. And they said, "These are your gods, O Israel, who brought you up out of the land of Egypt!" (Exodus 32:2, 4).

Not for a minute did Moses buy Aaron's lame alibi:

> And when Moses saw that the people had broken loose (for Aaron had let them break loose, to the derision of their enemies), then Moses stood in the gate of the camp and said, "Who is on the LORD's side? Come to me." And all the sons of Levi gathered around him (Exodus 32:25–26).

Verses 27–29 record how the Levites took swords to execute God's judgment pronounced by Moses. "The wages of sin is death" (Romans 3:23), always! Aaron's failure to handle the problem before it got out of hand cost three thousand Israelites their lives that day (Exodus 32:25-28).

Although the Levites would not formally become God's special priestly tribe until the first census in the book of Numbers, the golden calf calamity's correction was the first note of this idea. "And Moses said, 'Today you have been ordained for the service of the LORD, each one at the cost of his son and of his brother, so that he might bestow a blessing upon you this day'" (Exodus 32:29).

Despite his natural speaking ability and his being made Moses'
mouthpiece, Aaron has little to say the rest of the way. The whole book
of Leviticus about the Aaronic priesthood he led quotes him only once
(10:19). Chapter 10 opens with his oldest sons struck dead by God for
their sacrilege (Leviticus 10:1–3). These two comprised half of the next
level of priestly authority after their high priest father.

As Aaron's firstborn, Nadab was next in line to become a high
priest had he outlived his father. But the current high priest had failed
in training half of his lieutenants. He had not passed on to them a reverential fear of the holiness of God.

> *Now Nadab and Abihu, the sons of Aaron, each took his censer
> and put fire in it and laid incense on it and offered unauthorized
> fire before the Lord, which he had not commanded them. And
> fire came out from before the Lord and consumed them, and
> they died before the Lord. Then Moses said to Aaron, "This is
> what the Lord has said: 'Among those who are near me I will
> be sanctified, and before all the people I will be glorified.'" And
> Aaron held his peace (Leviticus 10:1–3).*

Moses was referring to what he would write as Exodus 19:20–22:

> *The Lord came down on Mount Sinai, to the top of the mountain.
> And the Lord called Moses to the top of the mountain, and Moses
> went up. And the Lord said to Moses, "Go down and warn the
> people, lest they break through to the Lord to look and many
> of them perish. Also let the priests who come near to the Lord
> consecrate themselves, lest the Lord break out against them"
> (Exodus 19:20–22).*

In Exodus 19:24, the Lord told Moses, "Go down, and come up bringing Aaron with you." Moses went down to give the people the oral version of the Ten Commandments. He invited seventy-three leaders to join him in a mid-mountain encounter with God:

Then Moses and Aaron, Nadab and Abihu, and seventy of the elders of Israel went up, and they saw the God of Israel. There was under his feet as it were a pavement of sapphire stone, like the very heaven for clearness. And he did not lay his hand on the chief men of the people of Israel; they beheld God, and ate and drank (Exodus 24:9–11).

What did God not raise His hand against? Something happened with this elite group to offend God's holiness and stir His wrath. But His grace prevailed. Perhaps some had too much to drink. Did they become irreverent or profane? God hints this in His rare direct address to priest Aaron, who had watched two cousins remove the corpses of his oldest sons:

And the LORD spoke to Aaron, saying, "Drink no wine or strong drink, you or your sons with you, when you go into the tent of meeting, lest you die. It shall be a statute forever throughout your generations. You are to distinguish between the holy and the common, and between the unclean and the clean, and you are to teach the people of Israel all the statutes that the LORD has spoken to them by Moses" (Leviticus 10:8–11).

Whatever the offense on the mount had been, Nadab and Abihu made a mental note of what a person could get away with in God's presence. This cavalier attitude cost them dearly in Leviticus 10. They lost their lives, and Aaron lost half his sons. But the details were not lost on Moses. He noticed that God was very strict when it came to people picking up the sacred censers. God could become incensed when the people involved in serving the Lord played with fire. Moses' mental note would come in handy later.

"Aaron held his peace" (Leviticus 10:3d) at Moses' insensitive synopsis of his sons' deaths and his intimation of their intoxication. Then Moses hits the play button for a four-verse version of the priests' obligation to eat on site the remains of the offering (10:12–15). When Moses chided Aaron's two remaining sons for not dining in, Aaron had all he could take:

> And Aaron said to Moses, "Behold, today they have offered their sin offering and their burnt offering before the LORD, and yet such things as these have happened to me! If I had eaten the sin offering today, would the LORD have approved?" And when Moses heard that, he approved (Leviticus 10:19–20).

Moses may have been content, for the time being, but Aaron was becoming discontent. Aaron was backsliding from augmenting Moses to arguing with Moses. The fault lines from Aaron's flaws would prove fatal for a whole generation of Israel.

CHAPTER 8

FLASHBACK

Faultlines were forming in Numbers 11–14. The storm did not suddenly appear out of nowhere. It had been brewing for weeks. This story did not start in Numbers 16. Korah's rebellion did not happen in a vacuum. The Hebrews enjoyed their first year out of Egyptian slavery, but then they began to lose patience. Negativity became the mood.

The story had progressed positively into Numbers chapter 11 if we view the golden calf incident (Exodus 32) as an aberration. Three factors converged to cause that hiccup. First was Moses' absence. Moses had been missing for forty days. He had his occasional mountaintop meeting with God but was usually back in camp after a week. This time, he had been away for more than a whole moon. Second, they did not yet have the tabernacle. In a world where all the other nations had visible gods, it was a challenge for the Hebrews to keep faith in God who was invisible. Once built, the tabernacle (God's house) gave them a tangible symbol of His presence. Third, they now had the Decalogue (the Ten Words or Ten Commandments). Though they were basically commands, the prologue reminded them that this whole deal was God's doing.

And God spoke all these words, saying: "I am the LORD your God, who brought you out of the land of Egypt, out of the house of slavery. You shall have no other gods before me" (Exodus 20:1–3).

But a new normal started in Numbers 10:11, where the story shifted gears. It had taken a year to move the Hebrews from Egypt to Mount Sinai to get the tabernacle built, and to organize the Levites. They observed Passover on the fourteenth day of the first month of the second year. That was exactly a year since the death angel passed over their abodes in Egypt, after seeing the blood of the lamb on their doorposts. Then the Tabernacle was raised up, accompanied by the Shekinah cloud, which conveyed God's presence and showed the Hebrews whether to linger or leave.

> *In the second year, in the second month, on the twentieth day of the month, the cloud lifted from over the tabernacle of the testimony, and the people of Israel set out by stages from the wilderness of Sinai. And the cloud settled down in the wilderness of Paran. They set out for the first time at the command of the* LORD *by Moses (Numbers 10:11–13).*

Now that moving into the Promised Land was finally off the back burner, things became hectic and hotter. First, moving was a hassle. Whenever the cloud departed, they had to pull up stakes and move everything in and through desert sand. The stakes got higher. They would agitate enemies, the current residents with squatter's rights. Even the vocabulary changes to military terminology. Peacetime moves are bad enough, but now they were armed and ready for attack. Things get suddenly serious.

> *They set out for the first time at the command of the* LORD *by Moses. The standard of the camp of the people of Judah set out first by their companies, and over their company was Nahshon the son of Amminadab (Numbers 10:13–14).*

The next fourteen verses use this same wording to parade the other eleven tribes to the front lines and call them to "forward, march!" (Numbers 10:15-28). Verse 28 adds this closing summary: "This was the order of march of the sons of Israel by their armies as they set out" (NASB).

Another military motif was the standards. Each of the twelve tribes had a different banner or ensign that identified them. But Israel marched in four companies of three tribes each. So for this march, only the lead tribe in each company raised its standard. Judah's standard led the first company, with the armies of Issachar and Zebulon following (Numbers 10:14–16).

Then the Levites carried the Tabernacle, followed by the standard of Reuben. Simeon and Gad joined in behind Reuben (10:17–20). Next, the Kohathite Levites carried the tabernacle furnishings. Then came the standards of Ephraim, with Manasseh and Benjamin, and the standard of Dan, with Asher and Naphtali (10:21–27).

There are periods of time when life gets more serious. We take on more responsibility. Events like going away to college, enlisting in the military, finding a first job, getting a new job, or receiving a promotion are some of these times. Getting married, becoming a parent, and answering God's vocational call to missions or ministry are other trying times. It was time for Israel to put their money where their mouth was. But they floundered. They freaked out. The pressure got to them. The wheels started coming off.

Between their first military march and Korah's rebellion six chapters later, there were **ten warning signs**. Ten slips, or missteps, or steps backward. Ten acts of unbelief. Ten times when faith was trumped by fear. Two of these were by Moses himself, one by Moses and Aaron, another by Moses' siblings, and one by his aide, Joshua. Three were by the whole congregation, or a majority of it. One was by an unnamed individual. Only one was by non-Hebrews outside the covenant, who knew not the Lord. The other nine were by covenant people who did know the Lord and should have known better. These ten harbingers of trouble begin to show the downward spiral:

1. Moses walked by sight, not faith (Numbers 10:29–32; 11:10–15, 21–23).
2. The people complained (Numbers 11:1–3).
3. The mixed multitude craved meat (Numbers 11:4–6, 31–34).
4. Moses crumbled to their complaints (Numbers 11:10–15, 21–23).
5. Jealous Joshua tried to quench the Spirit (Numbers 11:26–30).
6. Moses' siblings spoke out against him (Numbers 12:1–16).
7. Ten of the twelve spies gave a negative report (Numbers 13:1–33).
8. Moses and Aaron failed to exhort and encourage the people (Numbers 13:30–14:10).
9. The people voice-voted for the negative report (Numbers 14:1–4, 10).
10. The people tried to conquer Canaan themselves without the Lord (Numbers 14:39–45).

(1) Everything had gone great in the book of Numbers until a thought popped into Moses' head, which had not come from God. Moses failed to vet it with the Lord. But it seemed to him like a good idea, so he proceeded.

And Moses said to Hobab the son of Reuel the Midianite, Moses' father-in-law, "We are setting out for the place of which the LORD said, 'I will give it to you.' Come with us, and we will do good to you, for the LORD has promised good to Israel." But he said to him, "I will not go. I will depart to my own land and to my kindred." And he said, "Please do not leave us, for you know where we should camp in the wilderness, and you will serve as eyes for us. And if you do go with us, whatever good the LORD will do to us, the same will we do to you" (Numbers 10:29–32).

The above passage introduces a new name: Hobab. In Midian, Moses' father-in-law was known as Reuel, which means "friend of God." His being their priest (Exodus 2:16, 3:1) pictured this name and perhaps even occasioned it. But Moses always addressed him as Jethro (Exodus 3:1, 4:18, and seven times in Exodus 18). The term Jethro was how the Hebrews in Egypt had to refer to Pharaoh. Meaning "pre-eminence," Jethro was pre-eminent in his job (priest of Midian), as head of the new household Moses was moving into, and as Moses' new human authority instead of Pharaoh. But when Moses wrote Numbers 10:29, he reverted to Reuel for good reason. The Numbers 10:29 passage is about Hobab, not Jethro, so the reader needs to know how this new character fits into the story. "Reuel" was what Hobab called his father.

When Moses left Midian to return to Egypt as deliverer, his wife Zipporah and their two boys started out with him. But after God threatened to kill Moses for not circumcising their sons, she and the boys bailed out and backtracked to Reuel. When Reuel later heard that Moses and the Hebrews were safely out of Egypt and headed in his general direction, he delivered his daughter and grandsons to be reunited with Moses (Exodus 18:1–12). Reuel stayed long enough to see Moses wear himself out trying to solve everyone's problems. So he gave Moses a delegation plan that involved many people sharing the load. Reuel hoped this would leave Moses some time for his family (18:13–26). "Then Moses let his father-in-law depart, and he went away to his own country" (18:27).

Hobab was not a homebody but one who stayed on the go, like a Bedouin. Had he been living at home when Moses escaped to Midian, he would have been watering the sheep, instead of his sisters having to do what was considered man's work (Exodus 2:15–19). His travels and contacts kept him up on the news in the region. When he heard how the Hebrews had escaped Egypt under Moses' leadership and were on the move to Canaan, he hurried home to tell his sister and their father. Since Hobab knew the lay of the land, Reuel wisely enlisted him to guide them to Moses. But Hobab was not ready to settle down. When his father left to return home, Hobab stayed with his sister and pondered his next move. Moses asked him to stay and help guide the people.

Once Reuel left, Hobab and Zipporah were the only adult Midianites in the midst of millions of Hebrews. Their tent was a Midianite mobile home. Hobab liked her cooking, and she enjoyed his company. They had never spent much time together as brother and sister. Hobab had fun playing with Gershom and Eliezer. His nephews were fascinated with him and intrigued by his survival stories of life in the wild.

Zipporah liked having her big brother around, as there was much time when Moses was not. Even when Moses was present physically, he was absent minded. Moses was so preoccupied with managing and moving two million people in the desert that his mind was not on his family or their needs. Reuel had left, but Zipporah hoped Hobab would hang around even when the Hebrews started moving again. She had heard Reuel say what a great job his son did in guiding him through the desert and in anticipating where they would intersect with the Hebrew horde.

Being older with less stamina, Reuel appreciated that Hobab knew this desert well enough to know where its few oases were located. Reuel relished those rests in the shade, refueling his body with the cool, fresh liquid, and dates from the palm trees. Moses had told his wife what a challenge it had been to keep two million people hydrated in this arid area. So she would suggest that he invite her brother to accompany them when they broke camp.

God's cloud would show them when and where to move, but it had rarely routed them by water. "For we walk by faith, not by sight" (2 Corinthians 5:7) is in our Bible, but this had been a hard concept for Moses to master. Paul used a rare word in the above verse, *eidos*. It is found only four other times in Scripture, and only here is it translated "sight." The word means "appearance." But appearances can be deceiving, like a mirage.

It had appeared to Moses at the burning bush that Aaron would be a good spokesman for the message God called Moses to deliver. But the golden calf was the high price Moses paid for this crutch. Moses told Hobab that God was giving them the Promised Land. God did not need Hobab to help Him keep this promise. But Moses did, for he was walking by sight, not by faith.

(2) The people complained, again (Numbers 11:1–3). This Hebrew word *anan* means "to sigh habitually." It had become a habit. They were constantly murmuring. That word, *lun/lin*, had already been said of them ten times in the story before now. The first time was right after the Red Sea crossing. They could not drink the bitter water, so they complained against Moses (Exodus 15:24).

Although complaints are about something, they are usually against someone, whomever we blame for the problem. They murmured against Moses, or Moses and Aaron. Moses responded, "What are we, that you grumble against us?" (Exodus 16:7). And he reminded them in that same verse that God heard those complaints. God heard and hated their complaints (Exodus 16:7, 8, 9, 12), just as He hears and hates ours. By Numbers chapter 11, their number of complaints had exceeded God's grace:

And the people complained in the hearing of the LORD about their misfortunes, and when the LORD heard it, His anger was kindled, and the fire of the LORD burned among them and consumed some outlying parts of the camp. Then the people cried out to Moses, and Moses prayed to the LORD, and the fire died down. So the name of that place was called Taberah, because the fire of the LORD burned among them (Numbers 11:1–3).

Complaints tend to start in the outskirts of the group. Those at the core are too busy doing the work of the Lord to complain about the way it is being done. And they are the closest to hear whatever God says and see whatever He does. The more we are on fire for the Lord and fired up about how He is at work among us, the less the chance of our getting burned. Those who hang back and pass judgment are the most likely to do and say things to incur God's judgment.

(3) The mixed multitude craved meat (Numbers 11:4–6). In the account of the moment where the Hebrew slaves actually left Egypt, there is a one-verse notation that "a mixed multitude" departed with them (Exodus 12:38). In contrast to the majority of full-blooded Hebrew people starting their exodus, there was a minority mixed from other ethno-linguistic people groups, making their exit. The other biblical occurrence of this term, *ereb*, is centuries later in Nehemiah 13:3. It was another time when Hebrews were coming to Israel from a more powerful, populous country.

Such magnet nations attract people from smaller ones surrounding it. The recent devastation of the Ten Plagues had made Egypt a horrible place to live, but the Hebrews' God had been sheltering them with protection and showering them with provisions. Besides their flocks, herds, and a great deal of livestock, the Egyptians had loaded them with gold, silver, and clothing when they left. God's providential justice awarded this lump sum payment for their four centuries of slave labor. Leaving with the Hebrews emerged as an attractive option to staying and suffering with the Egyptians.

Translations such as the New International Version refer to this group as "the rabble." Our phrase, "rabble rousers," helps us understand how a mixed group lacking deep roots and strong ties can be easily swayed. Almost all Egypt's immigrants from elsewhere chose to emigrate with the Hebrews, as did some natives on the lower rungs of Egypt's socio-economic ladder. But the greener grass did not emerge quickly enough to suit them. They soon had second thoughts about having left. They soon forgot the many reasons they loathed Egypt and began to have idealistic longings for its few things they had liked. The term "multitude" means that they were a critical mass large enough to affect the majority, acting as a tipping point when momentum began to swing.

The modern mixed multitudes are people in churches for social, sociological, or socio-economic reasons. They are not born again, but they were born into the types of families that populate a particular church. Their kind of people go there, so they go with them. They lack the Holy Spirit within them, so they cannot comprehend spiritual things (1 Corinthians 2:11–14). They like the status quo, so they oppose any changes that would help reach more people. They are easily dissatisfied and quick to complain, which draws the sympathy and support of carnal Christians (1 Corinthians 3:1–3).

(4) Moses crumples at their complaints. The people had finally brought him down to their level. In this case, he does nothing to invite or exhort them to his level. He just blames God for it all:

Moses said to the LORD, "Why have you dealt ill with your servant? And why have I not found favor in your sight, that you lay the burden of all this people on me? Did I conceive all this people? Did I give them birth, that you should say to me, 'Carry them in your bosom, as a nurse carries a nursing child,' to the land that you swore to give their fathers? Where am I to get meat to give to all this people? For they weep before me and say, 'Give us meat, that we may eat.' I am not able to carry all this people alone; the burden is too heavy for me. If you will treat me like this, kill me at once, if I find favor in Your sight, that I may not see my wretchedness" (Numbers 11:11–15).

Our gracious God did not chide or rebuke Moses for this pity party pout. He merely moved to meet the felt need that Moses had stated. He let Moses choose seventy of the elders, on whom the Lord would put the same Spirit which was on Moses so they could help him bear the burden of the people. God also met the felt need the people stated, by giving them a month's supply of meat (Numbers 11:16–20). Moses should have thanked God for this and cheered up. But instead of letting the Lord lift him from his low, he continues to wallow in it:

But Moses said, 'The people among whom I am number six hundred thousand (soldiers) on foot, and you have said, 'I will give them meat, that they may eat a whole month!' Shall flocks and herds be slaughtered for them, and be enough for them? Or shall all the fish of the sea be gathered together for them, and be enough for them?" (Numbers 11:21–22).

(5) Jealous Joshua tried to quench God's Spirit:

Then the LORD came down in the cloud and spoke to him, and took some of the Spirit that was on him and put it on the seventy elders. And as soon as the Spirit rested on them, they prophesied.

But they did not continue doing it. Now two men remained in the camp, one named Eldad, and the other named Medad, and the Spirit rested on them. They were among those registered, but they had not gone out to the tent, and so they prophesied in the camp. And a young man ran and told Moses, "Eldad and Medad are prophesying in the camp." And Joshua the son of Nun, the assistant of Moses from his youth, said, "My lord Moses, stop them." But Moses said to him, "Are you jealous for my sake? Would that all the LORD's people were prophets, that the LORD would put his spirit on them!" (Numbers 11:25–29).

The Bible introduces Joshua in Exodus 17:9–13. The Amalekites attacked Israel, and Moses drafted Joshua to lead the battle. A principle of Bible interpretation called "the law of first reference" holds that its first mention of something can be a cue to Scripture's appraisal on the subject. Joshua tended to see things from a military perspective. By Exodus 24:13, Joshua is Moses' assistant and accompanies him up to the mountain of God.

When the two descended the mountain at the golden calf incident and got close enough to hear the people's howls, Joshua mistook them for war cries. But Moses knew this warfare was spiritual, and the shouts were from sin. Joshua seemed to be a loner who lacked people skills. In Exodus 33:7–11, Moses moved his "office" tent outside the camp, calling it "the tabernacle of meeting." The Lord would come down and meet with him there, and the people could go out to meet with Moses. "When Moses turned again into the camp, his assistant Joshua the son of Nun, a young man, would not depart from the tent" (Exodus 33:11).

Joshua would later be the one to succeed Moses as the top leader, but he was not quite ready for prime time. His jealousy of Eldad and Medad has a parallel in the gospels (Mark 9:38–40, Luke 9:49–50). Jesus rebuked John for wanting to stop someone not in the official twelve disciples from casting out demons in Jesus' name. Moses had a similar response to Joshua.

The gospel parallel came right after the disciples' dispute about which of them would be the greatest (Luke 9:46). Joshua being zealous for Moses' sake was a cloak for being zealous for his own renown. Joshua had gone from being one of only two people with God in the tabernacle of meeting to being one of seventy chosen elders who prophesied. Now there were two more men prophesying in the camp. Joshua had to nip this bud, lest the masses began to hop on the bandwagon, and the seventy be no longer elite. But like Jesus, Moses wanted as many people as possible to be speaking and acting for the Lord.

(6) Next, we have the account of Miriam and Aaron opposing their brother because he had married a Cushite woman. "Miriam and Aaron spoke against Moses because of the Cushite woman whom he had married; for he had married a Cushite woman" (Numbers 12:1). The momentum building against Moses infected even Moses' siblings. Mentioned first, Miriam was the instigator and the spokesperson. This was her idea and initiative, but she talked "Aaron Also" into accompanying her in this criticism.

Miriam had two bones to pick with their little brother, whom she thought was getting too big for his britches. Miriam thought she had become the Hebrews' first lady when God brought them through the Red Sea. She was at Moses' side when he raised his staff to part the waters, and then she got her few seconds in the spotlight. She would have called herself Moses' sister that day, but Scripture instead called her Aaron's.

Then Miriam the prophetess, the sister of Aaron, took a tambourine in her hand, and all the women went out after her with tambourines and dancing. And Miriam sang to them: "Sing to the LORD, for he has triumphed gloriously; the horse and his rider he has thrown into the sea" (Exodus 15:20–21).

Though Moses and Zipporah had been married for four decades in Midian, Miriam had never met her. Remember that Zipporah and her sons had started out with Moses when God called him back to Egypt as deliverer (Exodus 4:20). But a bloody incident at a lodging place on the way gave her a scare about Moses' God (Exodus 4:24–26), so Moses sent them back to her family (Exodus 18:1). They returned home while it was still close enough that she remembered the way and safe enough to risk traveling without a man.

The target of Miriam's tirade has been a mystery throughout history. Was Moses' wife a dark figure? Did she just have a tan or skin several tones darker than the Hebrews? Was it Zipporah? Or had she died or been divorced?

Scripture never names another wife for Moses, so this Numbers 12:1 woman is assumed to be Zipporah by most scholars. The King James Version and the New King James Version use the word "Ethiopian," suggesting very dark skin — but the Hebrew text says "Cushite." Cushite and Midianite are related terms, and the Cushites included descendants of Ham and Canaan.

Cushite does not necessarily mean black, and one translation is "fair of appearance." The rabbinical interpretation of Cushite is "beautiful." Miriam had saved her little brother's life when he was a baby. She had rarely seen him as he grew up in Egypt's palace and had never seen him during his four decades in Midian. Their reunion when he returned to Egypt was wonderful, and she was with him whenever she could find a reason or excuse.

It was a blow to Miriam's ego when Zipporah replaced her at Moses' side. If Zipporah's appearance lived up to its Cushite name as beautiful, this gave Miriam another reason to resent her. The ladies had followed Miriam, but now the men could not keep their eyes off Zipporah. Though Miriam despised Zipporah, the real root of her jealousy was Moses.

> *And they (Miriam and Aaron) said, "Has the LORD indeed spoken only through Moses? Has he not spoken through us also?" And the LORD heard it. Now the man Moses was very meek, more than all people who were on the face of the earth" (Numbers 12:2–3).*

Moses does not defend himself, but God does. God came down in the pillar of cloud, stood in the door of the tabernacle, and summoned Aaron and Miriam. He first mentioned but minimized their perceived role as prophets. "Hear my words: 'If there is a prophet among you ...'" (Numbers 12:6). Miriam had prophesied at the Red Sea but never before or since. Her prophecy was actually just a one-verse chorus or response to Moses' eighteen-verse praise. And her one verse was just a repeat of Moses' first verse. Aaron was just Moses' mouthpiece for whatever God had told Moses. God said He spoke to prophets in visions or dreams, but when He spoke plainly to Moses, face to face, Moses saw His form.

The Lord rebuked Moses' siblings for not being afraid to speak against Moses: "And the anger of the LORD was aroused against them, and he departed" (Numbers 12:9). When the cloud departed, Miriam became leprous. Aaron appealed to Moses on her behalf. Moses prayed for her healing. God refused. He shut her out of the camp for seven days, the standard sentence for any leper. The people wondered why their progress suddenly stopped for a week. And the word quickly spread that Miriam was to blame.

(7) Another misstep came when ten of the twelve spies sent to

spy out the Promised Land returned with a negative report (Numbers 13:25–33). Regrettably, this is one of the best-known Bible stories, needing little elaboration here. Its significance to the Korah story is its timing — it came in the chapters leading up to his rebellion. Had this not happened to open the door and pave the way, Korah may have lacked the motivation to consider this and the momentum to think it might work.

We are not told how or why Moses picked these dirty dozen spies or whether and how long he prayed about it. But each was a leader in his tribe. They spent forty days following Moses' instructions to a tee. They brought back fruit samples like Blue Ribbon winners at the county fair. But they spoke just one positive sentence (twenty words). Then, they bashed God's plan and promises with 124 words in ten sentences. They failed to mention the Lord, the power He had displayed in the past, and His promises for the future. "They brought the people of Israel a bad report" (Numbers 13:32).

(8) Moses and Aaron failed to exhort and encourage the people at this critical juncture (Numbers 13:30–14:10). If there was ever a *carpe diem* moment for these two top leaders to stand and speak out, this was it. Despite the negative discussion, "Caleb quieted the people before Moses and said, 'Let us go up at once and occupy it, for we are well able to overcome it'" (Numbers 13:30).

Once Caleb made the motion to proceed, Moses should have immediately seconded. He should have reminded the Hebrews how God had already delivered them from Egypt, a world power far superior to the Amalekites or the Anakim. But fear got Moses' tongue, and his silence opened the door for the naysayers to rebut Caleb's exhortation.

Although Caleb's plea was true, it was not theological. It was a good statement, but not a God statement. It fast-forwarded to the results (they could take possession of Canaan) but failed to focus on the reason (the

Lord had promised them the land and would keep His word). Caleb's heart knew and assumed this, but he failed to state it. "Faith comes from hearing, and hearing through the word of Christ" (Romans 10:17).

Moses should have finished Caleb's sentence, saying why they were well able to overcome Canaan — because God had said He would do this. Because Caleb's statement and Moses' silence left God out of the equation, the naysayers' knockout punch was that the Canaanite people were bigger and stronger than the Hebrew people.

(9) As a result of Moses' silence, the people voted for the bad report.

> *Then all the congregation raised a loud cry, and the people wept that night. And all the people of Israel grumbled against Moses and Aaron. The whole congregation said to them, "Would that we had died in the land of Egypt! Or would that we had died in this wilderness! Why is the LORD bringing us to this land, to fall by the sword? Our wives and our little ones will become a prey. Would it not be better for us to go back to Egypt?" And they said to one another, "Let us choose a leader and go back to Egypt"* (Numbers 14:1–4).

Moses and Aaron prostrated in prayer before the people. But Joshua and Caleb stood and spoke to the people. They tore their clothes in shame and corporate repentance. This time they did focus their exhortation on how the Lord would deliver His people, so there was no need to fear the Canaanites. But it was too little, too late. The tipping point had already turned in the wrong direction. "Then all the congregation said to stone them with stones" (Numbers 14:10a).

We never know how long our windows of opportunity to trust and obey the Lord will remain open. This time God had heard enough, His patience ran out, and He slammed the window and locked it. He pronounced a forty-year death sentence in the wilderness for every Hebrew over age twenty, except Caleb and Joshua (Numbers 14:10b–39).

(10) Realizing the mess they had made, the people tried to conquer Canaan themselves without the Lord. Human beings are prone to pendulum reactions. The night before, they refused to attack Canaan with the Lord. The morning after, they had a change of heart, and showed up ready to go. Moses tried to dissuade them. He explained that to go now (after God had sentenced them to die in the wilderness) would be as disobedient as was their refusal to enter Canaan with God when He said to go.

> And they rose early in the morning and went up to the heights of the hill country, saying, "Here we are. We will go up to the place that the LORD has promised, for we have sinned." But Moses said, "Why now are you transgressing the command of the LORD, when that will not succeed? Do not go up, for the LORD is not among you, lest you be struck down before your enemies. For there the Amalekites and the Canaanites are facing you, and you shall fall by the sword. Because you have turned back from following the LORD, the LORD will not be with you." But they presumed to go up to the heights of the hill country, although neither the ark of the covenant of the LORD nor Moses departed out of the camp. Then the Amalekites and the Canaanites who lived in that hill country came down and defeated them and pursued them, even to Hormah (Numbers 14:40-45).

Bottomed Out

When the bottom falls out, it can reopen old wounds from our past. Officiating hundreds of funerals, with the bereavement ministry that accompanies this, I've seen the deceased's closest survivors have old griefs resurface to join this new one. Fresh grief floods us with false guilt. We think of something we said or did — or that we failed to do — which may have offended our loved ones in their last days.

In such emotional stress, our mind replays our relationship with our deceased, but in a very idealistic way. It replays it as though meeting the loved ones' needs or requests was the only responsibility we had in life and that we were the only person on earth who could do things for them. These guilt feelings may be intensified if they are from the last days of your loved one's life. We think, "If I had only known the time was so short." But you did not know, and your care and comfort had to be stretched over the long haul. You did what you thought was the best and most loving thing at the time.

Battling Back

Jesus gave His disciples great insights on this on the evening before He died for them. Knowing that even the best human comfort will fall short, He referred them to the Comforter, who is the Holy Spirit (John 14:16, 26; 15:26, 16:7, NIV).

"Comforter," "counselor" and "helper" are the best translations of the Greek word, *paraclete*, a compound word meaning "called alongside of." God the Father and God the Son have called the Holy Spirit alongside those who know the Lord to help, guide, and comfort us. So call Him alongside you when you need Him in these ways.

Jesus notes some ways the Comforter will help in our grief. First, we have His abiding presence and company "to be with you forever, even the Spirit of truth" (John 14:16–17). As you experience His presence and pour out your heart to Him, He will give you a truer picture of how you cared for your loved one and how the Spirit is caring for you. Second, our Advocate will teach you all things and remind you of which words of Jesus will help you at critical times (14:26). Third, He will give us a testimony, as He testifies of Jesus' love for you and guides and strengthens you on how to testify for Him (15:26–27). Finally, He gives us righteousness to bring you to understand the right things about your loved one's living, dying, and death and to be at peace with the conscientious care you gave him or her. "He will bring to your remembrance" (14:26).

Here's how I have often seen the Holy Spirit's comfort when a believer has lost a loved one. Your memory is flooded with the hard times for you and your loved one in their suffering and in their dying, and your hard times then and since. A big way the Holy Spirit comforts you is to recede these painful memories to the back of your mind while He returns to the top of your head your mental picture of your loved one from the joyful periods in your life together.

CHAPTER 9

THE NIGHT BEFORE
THE MORNING AFTER

The day before the showdown at sunup ends at Numbers 16:17. A chapter break would have been helpful here, but most Bible versions do not even start a new paragraph. First-time or casual readers would tend to keep reading straight through, not realizing there has been a sunset and a sunrise between verses 17 and 18.

Verse 18 begins a new day, one of the most action-packed days in the Bible. A day like none before or since. It changed forever the lives of a million people. The day before had been long, eventful, stressful, and exhausting for everyone involved. Let's review the cast of characters introduced in that day's fray and surmise how they might have spent the night.

On is the fourth person the chapter names, even before Moses and Aaron, but his role was just a cameo. He was on and off the stage quickly. He is never mentioned again, either in this event or anywhere in the Bible. It appears that his appearance was spontaneous.

As his fellow Reubenites walked by his tent, On may have asked Dathan and Abiram where they were going. They replied that they were on their way to speak with Moses and that he could go along with them. A nobody like On jumped at the chance to visit with somebody like Moses. But he would not jump on their bandwagon. When he heard the words and tone of their opening salvo against Moses and Aaron, he wanted no part of this. Without saying a word, he turned away and returned to his tent and his family.

Moses did not mention On when he summoned Dathan and Abiram to return (Numbers 16:12). On is not mentioned in their reply to Moses (16:13–14). He is not named in Moses' return visit to them (16:25), nor when Moses warns the people to get away from their tents (16:24, 27).

(*See note at chapter's end for how a Jewish writing that credits On's wife for getting him out of Korah's rebellion, but the scenario above seems to fit Scripture better.)

It appears that Moses and the Lord realized that On had gotten in before he knew what was happening and got out quickly once he realized what was. First Corinthians 10:1–12 cites this general period of Old Testament history, stating that these things happened as examples to us for our admonition. Verse 13 promises that, with every temptation, God will make a way of escape. Had On stayed with Moses' critics a moment longer, he may have passed the point of no return. But he recognized and resisted the temptation and took the way of escape before the exit door closed. So the night before the morning after would have been just business as usual for On: a restful sleep.

Korah's co-conspirators with Dathan and Abiram were big shots ... men of renown ... 250 leaders of the congregation. They are numbered but not named. All the tribes were represented, so there were twenty or so per tribe. Three tribes lived on each side of the tabernacle, so they headed in four directions to start their walk home. The lead tribe in each direction got home first since their tents pitched closest to the tabernacle. As the next tribe reached home, their rearward tribe kept going.

The mass walkout began in silence, as nobody knew what to say. But as each tribe's leaders re-entered their own borders, they stopped for a brief tribal council, before heading for their tents. They had to recap what happened that day and rehearsed what was coming tomorrow and how to prepare. As they scattered to their tents, each man had little time to think through how much he would share with his family, or how little. So there were a dozen versions in each tribe.

It was getting late. The meals were ready, and their families were waiting. As they finished dinner, the wife would broach the conversation. Her icebreaker was something like, "How did your day go?" The typical male response was, "Okay." It was only the women who kept asking more pointed follow-up questions who got a hint of the gravity of the situation.

It may have happened this way: Before these 250 retired for the night, each made a silent search. They were to bring their censers the next day. They would not have time to scurry around at daybreak looking for them, so each made a quick visual check to make certain his censer was there. This family fire pan should be at the fireplace, just outside the tent door. But sometimes these got borrowed and not returned before dark, or the children might have played with them and forgot to put them back in place. Once each of the 250 had verified that his censer was there or found it elsewhere, the leader and his family retired for the night.

Aaron did not know what to make of the situation. His tent was close by the tabernacle, but he wanted a little exercise before he faced his family. So "Aaron Also" stopped by sister Miriam's on the way home to run the day's events by her and get her take. Being the firstborn, she tended to be critical of her little brothers, but usually behind their backs. Aaron was in her face, so this left Moses as tonight's target for her backstabbing. Aaron would try to reconstruct what had been said and done that day. At first it was a blur. But as Aaron caught his breath and

concentrated harder, Korah's opening shot at Moses and Aaron rever-
berated in his recall. "You have gone too far! For all in the congregation
are holy, every one of them, and the LORD is among them. Why then do
you exalt yourselves above the assembly of the LORD?" (Numbers 16:3).

Aaron had not memorized the words verbatim. But it had been such
a stinging salvo that he was able to paraphrase it well enough to give
Miriam the gist. This was enough to ignite her indignation. But even the
harshest criticisms contain a grain of truth. Miriam knew Korah's crew
was correct about Moses' failure to share leadership. Delegation was a
leadership skill missing from Moses' toolbox. His father-in-law Jethro
was the first to confront Moses about this and give him a delegation
plan (Exodus 18:13–27). Moses tried this for a while, but then slipped
back into his old ways.

Miriam recalled how the Lord had recently remediated this with the
seventy elders (Numbers 11:16–17). Two things had etched this in her
memory. First, this glass ceiling had shut her out, as all these new elders
were male. Second, when the Lord transferred to the elders some of the
Spirit that was upon Moses, they prophesied (Numbers 11:24–30). She
had been "the prophetess" (Exodus 15:20), a very exclusive title. There
were now seventy new prophets, and she was excluded from this fresh
manifestation.

Miriam bit her tongue to blanket her bitterness. But picking up on
Korah's charge, she asked Aaron whether Moses had summoned the
seventy as evidence against the accusation. This is what she, the prophetess, would have done had she been present or consulted. Aaron hung
his head and mumbled that Moses had not even mentioned this new
level of leaders.

Miriam was mortified. She could not believe her ears. How could
Moses overlook such a recent example? Maybe Korah was right that
Moses and Aaron had taken everything upon themselves. But what

if things got out of hand, and their coup grew to an assassination of Moses and Aaron? What if they lopped the whole Amram branch off the family tree?

Miriam morphed from criticism to self-preservation. Her tent was right behind Moses and Aaron's and just outside the tabernacle entrance, where the community meetings were held. So she would rise at the crack of dawn and spend her day visiting the perimeters of the camp to avoid becoming collateral damage.

It was getting dark. Aaron had to get home to Elisheba and their sons. Eleazer and Ithamar had survived their siblings, Nadab and Abihu. Elisheba was much more into cooking than conversation. Aaron spent the whole dinnertime praising the chef and her cuisine. Once the restaurant closed, the family retired for the night. Aaron's stomach was full, but his spiritual tank was empty.

Dathan and Abiram were brothers, so they were next-door neighbors. Father Eliab's tent was just before theirs in the Reubenite region. They had been home most of the day. They had accompanied Korah to the tabernacle entrance, expecting a discussion and a democratic decision. But Moses had played the spiritual card and prostrated himself before the Lord. They got tired of waiting for some action and grew impatient. They did not do prayer meetings, so they headed home.

When Moses got up, they were conspicuous by their absence. They had stood right beside Korah, giving moral support as he stood up to Moses and Aaron. Moses sent to collect them back, but they refused this collect call. They gave as strong and long a defense as the messenger would remember to be relayed back to Moses. Angered by this insubordination in their refusal to return, Moses' quick response was to the Lord: "Do not respect their offering." This curse would quickly pass, or pass muster, at the showdown at sunup.

Moses was exhausted. Twenty-twenty hindsight hit him in the head.

He realized in retrospect that he should have summoned the seventy new elders, once Korah leveled his charge that Moses and Aaron led like dictators. The new elders were evidence against this — a recent rebuttal. This was the first thought which had popped into his head, but as it moved to his mouth, his eyes hit the brakes. He had glimpsed two of these elders in the row behind Korah, and he feared there may be more. This disappointment shocked and socked him. Its impact immobilized him, and he crumpled to the dust. Was there anyone he could depend on and still trust? The Lord! Moses switched from defense to offense. Continuing in the prone position, he prostrated himself in prayer. The Lord received him, reassured him, and rewarded him with the response plan.

Once the confrontation ended, everyone retreated to their tents with the battle lines drawn. Moses' tent was just a stone's throw. He set his gaze and started his feet in that direction. He was refreshed by Zipporah's warm welcome and delicious dinner. He gave her a recap of the day. He had to let her know about Korah's rebellion. Zipporah had already had bad vibes about Korah, but Dathan and Abiram were new names to her. Moses did not dare mention the 250 leaders who showed up to back up this trio. He related how his long prayer time with God had boosted his spirits. Moses outlined the plan the Lord had revealed for the next day. The day would be long and maybe the most eventful day since the Red Sea crossing. Moses would need his strength. They summoned their sons, prayed as a family, and retired for the night.

Korah was frustrated. The day had not gone as planned. Korah had been planning this for a while. He actually had five plans, five possible outcomes he could envision. Plan E was Egypt, if he could push Moses into fleeing there. Since Pharaoh had drowned in the Red Sea and his son had died with the firstborn, Moses was now actually the legal successor to their throne. He grew up in the palace, as Pharaoh's adopted grandson. There was good precedent for a Hebrew running Egypt as Joseph had worked wonders in a prior crisis. The Egyptians had seen Moses' power, which could help them rebuild their country. Korah's Plan B for Moses was sending him back to Midian. Moses had been happy there and had left only reluctantly. He had a good relationship with Jethro and Hobab. Zipporah would jump at this option.

Korah's Plan A was Aaron. He had been Moses' Achilles heel since the golden calf episode. Aaron's recent performance had undermined whatever confidence Moses may have had left in him. Korah was a Levite, as close kin to Levi and Kohath as were Aaron and Moses. If their confrontation had become negotiation, Korah would have bargained to take Aaron's place in return for calling off the dogs. Plan D was delegation. Had Moses promised to share collegial leadership with the seventy new elders and commit to some specific conditions Korah would require, there could be peaceful coexistence.

Plans A-B-D-E would have been bloodless and would have left the common people alone. But it had come down to Plan C: catastrophe. Moses had forfeited the four compromise peace plans, which everyone could have lived with. Now, calamity was coming. This outcome would result in winners and losers. Some might even lose their lives, depending on whether and how God intervened.

Moses loved to claim the high road. The Lord did not always show up for Moses, but He never showed up against him. If God chose to sit this one out, Korah was confident. He had the numbers and the momentum. In all of the day's dialogues, there was only one word that kept Korah up that night: censers. Censers had been involved when his nephews Abihu and Nadab had died. But they had offered strange unauthorized fire on their own, not authorized by Israel's high priest Aaron or God's spokesman, Moses. Since Moses had called for tomorrow's censers, there should be no problem or penalty. At least that's what Korah was hoping. He had been running on adrenalin for days, and his exhausted body finally demanded sleep.

The night before the morning after seemed the longest for a trio of brothers not in that day's cast of characters: Assir, Elkanah, and Abiasaph. They had always been close in age and activity, enjoying their horizontal relationship. What bothered them tonight was one vertical relationship in the family tree. They were the sons of Korah (Exodus 6:24).

Their father had been uptight lately. He had been hanging with a couple of Reubenites. But whenever they stumbled upon him discussing Dathan and Abiram with Mom, the topic of conversation quickly changed. Like many fathers, theirs had been away all day. Their dinner table was eerily quiet that night. So they ate quickly, then asked to be excused. They mentioned the youth get-together on the other side of the camp.

But once they were out of sight, they made a U-turn back to their tent. They had discovered a safe spot behind the tent where they could eavesdrop on their parents' conversation. What they overheard that night sent chills down their spine. Korah was leading a mutiny against the leadership of their uncles, Moses and Aaron. He had enlisted hundreds of leaders from the twelve tribes. They confronted Moses and Aaron that day. Moses had not backed down, so things would come to a head the next day. A showdown at sunup!

It *May* Have Happened This Way

Assir motioned for his younger brothers, who had always looked up to him. He led them out of earshot of their parents. They had to vent their shock to one another and make some quick decisions on what to do the next day. Elkanah and Abiasaph thought Assir was overreacting. Father had always talked big, so maybe this would just blow over. They wanted to sleep on it and explore their options tomorrow. Assir said tomorrow might be too late. They had always tried to honor their father and mother, especially since God had made this the fifth of the Ten Commandments. But it had long been obvious that God was on Uncle Moses' side. What if their familial duty to honor their father and their faith dedication to follow Uncle Moses as Israel's appointed and anointed leader became mutually exclusive?

Assir suggested they go to Aunt Miriam's tent to spend the night. They were always welcome there. But Elkanah and Abiasaph said that Father would come looking for them, if they did not return to their tent. Assir was outvoted. If they went home without him, Korah would be mad. Assir reluctantly gave in but warned Elkanah and Abiasaph that he would wake them up first thing in the morning, for a quick decision.

It was dark when they got back to their tent. Korah had retired for the night, but Mother was at the tent door, waiting for them. The three quietly slipped to their corner, lest they awaken Korah. Assir laid his body down, but his mind kept racing. He had thought through various plans of action or inaction, calculating their consequences, and weighing the options. He vacillated between strategies.

The natural thing would be to stay silent and remain at home. But he felt a tug in his spirit, the Lord drawing him to desert his father *if* Korah continued to defy Israel's God-appointed leader. Assir concluded that the safest plan spiritually was to slip out and side with Uncle Moses, even if he had to face a furious father. He was about to whisper this conclusion to his brothers, but they were already snoring.

Assir envied their ability to shut this out and go to sleep. But his mind would not let go of the dilemma he faced at dawn. So he spent the night in prayer, begging for the Lord to make the decision for him. Tomorrow this son would be forced to pull the trigger on the most monumental decision of his life.

The Midrash (Midrash Hagadol, Bamidbar 16:32) says that On ben Pelet was rescued by his wife. When he returned home and told her he was taking part in the revolt, she argued, "What do you gain of it? Your position will be the same, whether Aaron or Korah is the High Priest." He agreed with her logic but explained that he couldn't disengage from Korah since he had sworn to join their rebellion the next morning.

So she mixed a strong drink to put him to sleep. Then she uncovered her hair and sat at the tent entrance. When Korah sent messengers to summon On, they turned back at the immodest sight of On's wife. When death struck Korah and his followers, On's bed began to move. His wife gripped it and prayed to God for her husband's forgiveness.

After On was spared, his wife urged him, "Now go apologize to Moses!" When On refused due to his embarrassment, his wife approached Moses, weeping and begging for his forgiveness. Moses then personally went to On's tent and encouraged him, saying, "Come out! May the Almighty forgive you!"

For the rest of his life, On mourned and repented for his sin, thankful for the miracle of being spared thanks to his wife's wisdom. On's name reflects this. On means "mourning," since he was in a state of mourning. Ben Pelet means "a son *(ben)*, or man, who was rescued from destruction by a miracle *(pele)*."

On's wife convinced her husband not to join Korah by explaining that he was not a high priest and would never become one. She understood that, despite our best intentions in using physical reality for higher service, we need the hierarchy of the High Priest to remind us of our priorities. (*"The Jewish Woman," article cdo/aid/396440, www.chabad.org.*)

CHAPTER 10

SHOW UP FOR SHOWDOWN

So every man [of the 250 who confronted Moses and Aaron the day before] took his censer and put fire in them and laid incense on them and stood at the entrance of the tent of meeting with Moses and Aaron. Then Korah assembled all the congregation against them [Moses and Aaron] at the entrance of the tent of meeting. And the glory of the LORD appeared to all the congregation (Numbers 16:18–19).

Remember that verse 18 happens a sunset and a sunrise after verse 17. None of the participants and spectators could have forgotten. Because Moses would not surrender to Korah's rebellion the day before, and Korah's crew would not back off, we now have a showdown at sunrise. D-Day had dawned.

The human authors of the sixty-six books of the Bible did not divide them into chapters and verses. This was done centuries after the last New Testament book had been written. But Moses used a literary device to alert those reading Numbers in Hebrew that it is a new day. He injected a different word for "congregation" than he had used exclusively for this group in his 16:1–17 account of the day before. The Hebrew word, *moed*, means "a meeting place" or "the meeting itself." Moses opted for *moed* in the two verses printed above and three times later in the chapter.

Because this word meant "meeting place," it was always used when referencing the tabernacle of the congregation. The primary Hebrew word for "congregation" is *edah*, which Moses uses a dozen times in this chapter. The Hebrew language has fewer words than New Testament Greek or even our English, so Moses also used *edah* for Korah's company five times in this chapter, and he used *edah* for "assembly" in Numbers 16:2.

The writer of Psalm 106 used *edah* twice for "company" in the three-verse recap of this incident:

> *"When men in the camp were jealous of Moses and Aaron, the holy one of the* LORD, *the earth opened and swallowed up Dathan, and covered the company of Abiram. Fire also broke out in their company; the flame burned up the wicked" (Psalm 106:16–18).*

This psalm adds weight and insight to Moses' accounts of Korah's rebellion. Since this psalm also recounts incidents long after Moses, it was written by someone else. It thus fulfills the biblical requirement "that every charge may be established by the evidence of two or three witnesses" (Matthew 18:16, 2 Corinthians 13:1, Deuteronomy 17:6). The Psalm 106 writer is the second witness, and Jude 11 is the third.

This psalmist's insight is "Aaron, the holy one of the Lord." Aaron is called this not because of his own righteousness, as Scripture records some of his gross sins. He was the holy one because Aaron was the one the Lord chose, appointed, and anointed as high priest. Korah had failed to grasp this in his claim that "all in the congregation are holy, every one of them" (Numbers 16:3). Moses immediately fell on his face (16:4), realizing how this statement would offend God, who might zap Korah on the spot.

Moses' next spoken words to Korah and all his company empha-sized the singularity and exclusivity the Lord had built into the high priest position:

"In the morning the LORD will show who is his, and who is holy, and will bring him near to him. The one whom he chooses he will bring near to him. … the man whom the LORD chooses shall be the holy one" (Numbers 16:5, 7).

High priest was a solo position for a solo person. It was God who chose Aaron as the first person in this position — an early example of the biblical doctrine of election. God further chose that after the very first high priest, a high priest would be succeeded by his oldest surviving son, who had not disqualified himself.

This came into play centuries later when "the sons of Eli were worthless men. They did not know the LORD" (1 Samuel 2:12). God allowed them to be killed in battle for sacrilegiously treating the Ark of the Covenant like a good luck charm (1 Samuel 4:4–11). Eli died hearing this news, and God chose to pass the high priesthood to Eli's adopted son, Samuel. Samuel had grown up within the tribe of Ephraim (1 Samuel 1:1), but he was genetically a Levite and actually a son of Korah.

Hebrews in the New Testament echoes the divine authority God has vested in the call and ministry of the shepherds leading His flocks:

Remember your leaders, those who spoke to you the word of God. Consider the outcome of their way of life and imitate their faith. … Obey your leaders and submit to them, for they are keeping watch over your souls, as those who will have to give an account. Let them do this with joy and not with groaning, for that would be of no advantage to you. … Now may the God of peace who brought again from the dead our Lord Jesus, the great shepherd of the sheep, by the blood of the eternal covenant, equip you with everything good that you may do his will, working in us

*that which is pleasing in his sight, through Jesus Christ, to whom
be glory forever and ever. Amen (Hebrews 13:7, 17, 20–21).*

After the ominous night before the morning after, who would show
up for the showdown at sunup?

Moses and Aaron were hosting the showdown, so they are the
first named as showing up for it. Moses had a word from the Lord
and the peace of God that when the showdown ended, he would still
be the leader. "Aaron also" figured that if Moses felt good about the
day's prospects, he could too. Korah's company, the 250 leaders of the
congregation, reported as instructed. Not a single man was missing. The
leaders were front and center; Korah was opposite of Moses and Aaron.

The fourth person named individually at the show-up for showdown
was the Lord. "And the glory of the Lord appeared to all the congregation" (Numbers 16:19b). It had not appeared to the congregation on
the day before. He had not manifested Himself publicly. He had only
revealed Himself privately to Moses. There were times that day when
Moses spoke *to* the Lord, and times he spoke *for* the Lord. God was also
symbolically present in the tabernacle. The Lord was in earshot of the
conversations, but He was to be seen and heard that day just by faith,
not by eye or ear.

When God shows up, He does not come to take sides. Decades later,
with the Hebrews finally poised to enter the Promised Land, Moses'
successor Joshua still struggled with this mentality. Near Jericho, the
huge walled city facing the Israelites as they entered Canaan, he would
encounter God's glory in the form of a warrior with drawn sword.
Joshua knew this was not one of his men, and he ruled out this being a
sentry or scout from Jericho.

Joshua approached this mighty warrior with holy fear, getting up
the nerve to ask, "Are you for us, or for our adversaries?"

The answer was:

"No; but I am the commander of the army of the LORD. Now I have come." And Joshua fell on his face to the earth and worshiped and said to him, "What does my lord say to his servant?" And the commander of the LORD's army said to Joshua, "Take off your sandals from your feet, for the place where you are standing is holy." And Joshua did so (Joshua 5:14–15).

No, God does not come to take sides. He comes to take over. He comes to take charge. God does not fight His own people, so it was not a celestial soldier who showed up for Korah's showdown at sunup. The *shekinah* glory cloud glowed with majestic brilliance. It moved slowly but stately from high atop the center of the tabernacle to a lower position just above its entrance. Its easternmost edge eclipsed Moses and Aaron, who stood just outside the door, facing their 250 challengers.

The day before, the confederates counted the Lord on their side and counted on the Lord:

They assembled themselves together against Moses and against Aaron and said to them, "You have gone too far! For all in the congregation are holy, every one of them, and the LORD is among them. Why then do you exalt yourselves above the assembly of the LORD?" (Numbers 16:3).

Moses had gone them one better. He could have argued with them about whose side the Lord was on. But he simply and serenely stated that God would show up the next morning to resolve the matter (Numbers 16:5).

God would have little to say on this fateful day. He spoke only three times (16:20–21, 23–24, 36–38) and never to the congregation. He began with one dreadful sentence to Moses and Aaron, a death sentence for the congregation:

> *And the glory of the* LORD *appeared to all the congregation. And the* LORD *spoke to Moses and to Aaron, saying, "Separate yourselves from among this congregation, that I may consume them in a moment" (Numbers 16:19b–21).*

Dathan and Abiram were no-shows for Scene One of *Show Up at Showdown.* But God had not forgotten them. His mind still saw them there on the front row of yesterday's protest. They would experience what Jonah would learn centuries later. When you start something with God, or He starts something with you, "You can run, but you can't hide."

> *And the* LORD *spoke to Moses, saying, "Say to the congregation, Get away from the dwelling of Korah, Dathan, and Abiram." Then Moses arose and went to Dathan and Abiram" (Numbers 16:23–25).*

Nobody else is named in Scene One of the *Show Up for Showdown.* But I can envision three other people there, in the shadows. As Korah made the momentous march that morning from his tent to God's tent, I picture his sons following at a distance. Assir may have wakened his brothers Elkanah and Abiasaph once their father had headed for the showdown. Within minutes they would be on his trail. They could catch sight of him just before he reached the tabernacle. I picture them just behind the 250, out of Korah's sight line, but close enough for them to see and hear what would transpire.

What *edah* (congregation) was God about to consume? God is a consuming fire (Deuteronomy 4:24, 9:3, Hebrews 12:29). How widespread and inclusive was this death sentence? Did God mean just the 250 rebels who congregated against Moses and Aaron for the second straight day at the tabernacle entrance? Or did He mean the whole congregation of Israel (besides Moses and Aaron and their families)?

Would God wipe out two million people because of what a tenth of 1 percent of them had said and done those two days? Over ninety-nine and ninety-eight one hundredths of the Hebrews had stayed home that fateful day, minding their own business. As their father Abraham had asked the Lord about Sodom, "Will you indeed sweep away the righteous with the wicked?" (Genesis 18:23). What light do biblical precedent, Hebrew vocabulary, and the details recorded on this incident shed on the scope of the congregation whose destruction God had declared?

On what group had God just pronounced a death sentence to be executed that day? Biblical precedent, in two of the three Bible books before Numbers, allows the maximum answer. The Genesis flood exterminated the entire human race except for one family of eight people.

The Tower of Babel may have been a justification to wipe out most of humanity again. But instead, God made a drastic, strategic change in how He related to the human race.

Starting with Adam and again with Noah, God had been rebuffed twice in His gracious attempts to be all-inclusive, relating directly to all people. Dealing comprehensively with all of earth's inhabitants had failed to advance His kingdom agenda for His world. For the rest of the Old Testament, God would contract and covenant with the family of one man, Abraham, who descended from Noah's son, Shem. God would change his covenant name to Abr(ah)am in Genesis chapter 17, but He outlines the strategy in His earlier call to Abram:

Now the LORD said to Abram, "Go from your country and your kindred and your father's house to the land that I will show you.

And I will make of you a great nation, and I will bless you and make your name great, so that you will be a blessing. I will bless those who bless you, and him who dishonors you I will curse, and in you all the families of the earth shall be blessed" (Genesis 12:1–3).

The Bible's second book, Exodus, records an incident that incensed the Lord against "the congregation" of His covenant people. Moses had been atop Mount Sinai forty days with God. He had received two tablets of stone, with the Ten Commandments carved by God, and detailed plans for the tabernacle the Hebrews were to build.

Before Moses had any human awareness of the disaster below, God gave him a quick summary. God told Moses what had happened, how it had offended Him, and how they had worn out His patience:

And the Lord said to Moses, "Go down, for your people, whom you brought up out of the land of Egypt, have corrupted themselves. They have turned aside quickly out of the way that I commanded them. They have made for themselves a golden calf and have worshiped it and sacrificed to it and said, 'These are your gods, O Israel, who brought you up out of the land of Egypt!'" And the LORD said to Moses, "I have seen this people, and behold, it is a stiff-necked people. Now therefore let me alone, that my wrath may burn hot against them and I may consume them, in order that I may make a great nation of you" (Exodus 32:7–10).

In the golden calf incident, God stated the truth that the people had abandoned His way, trading Him on the cheap for an artificial god. Since He created humanity with free will, He would not force their fealty to Him. He would continue to narrow the scope of the human agents through whom He would work His plan. God weeds out those who refuse to trust and obey. He has been downsizing. God is a consuming fire (Hebrews 12:29), and he is willing to eradicate this entire congregation, save one family.

But remembering His promises to Abraham, God hints to Moses that there is a way to mitigate His wrath. Unless Moses intervenes, God will consume this people, except for Moses' branch on Abraham's family tree. In response, Moses does intervene and intercedes (Exodus 32:11–13). "And the LORD relented from the disaster that he had spoken of bringing on his people" (Exodus 32:14). But "the wages of sin is death" (Romans 6:23).

Once Moses was back down with the people, he was disgusted as he saw for himself the gravity of their sin. As their human spiritual leader, Moses executed a death sentence. Three thousand individuals paid the wages of death for this corporate sin. These three thousand were not in the group when the Levites answered Moses' call for volunteers to deal with this situation. Sanctified imagination suggests that, in God's sovereignty, the three thousand who died included the individual instigators of the idolatry. The rest were the revelers who indulged in the immorality ignited by the idolatry.

These biblical precedents up the stakes for the "Show Up for Showdown." When God told Moses and Aaron to separate themselves from the congregation so that He could consume them, God could have meant the whole congregation. The exception was the descendants of Amram. His sons, Moses and Aaron, were given advance notice to flee the coming destruction (Numbers 16:20–21).

Hebrew vocabulary sheds light on the scope of this death sentence. Exodus 32:9–10 is the passage that most parallels Numbers 16:20–21, but the former omits the word congregation. Instead, Exodus 32:9 twice uses the common Hebrew word, *am,* for "people." The congregation

God threatened to destroy in Numbers 16:21 was *edah*, an appointed meeting.

In addition to the Hebrew word *moed*, Numbers 16 also uses *qahal* ("an assembly called together"). English meanings of all three words tilt toward this divine death sentence pronounced on just the smaller group. The 250 or so in this assembly called together (the "appointed meeting" at "this meeting place" or "the meeting itself") had crossed the line with God. 1 John 5:16 calls this "a sin leading to death" and says intercession is too late for such. Numbers 16 appears to use *qahal* for the whole congregation of Israel, those remaining once the ringleaders were swallowed alive by the pit and perished from among the assembly. This refers to what was left of the nation of Israel after Korah, Dathan, and Abiram vanished.

Moses was not just the biblical writer of this narrative but a main character in it. The way he quotes himself in verse 22 shows that he understood God's judgment to have been pronounced on just the 250 rebels and not on the whole nation. "O God, the God of the spirits of all flesh, shall one man sin, and will you be angry with all the congregation."

The one man was Korah, whom the New Testament gives full blame (Jude 11). Moses appealed for mercy on the 250 who had been incited by Korah. By reducing the guilt to the one in charge, Moses would have been willing to forgive even Dathan and Abiram. But God was not, choosing not to override the angry curse Moses had pronounced on them the day before (16:15). God agreed that Korah was ground zero for his waiting wrath. But this pebble in the pond would ripple out to rock not just Dathan and Abiram but even the 250 leaders misled by Korah.

CHAPTER 11

NEW THING/OLD HAT: MOSES

"There is nothing new under the sun" (Ecclesiastes 1:9).

"Behold, I am doing a new thing; now it springs forth" (Isaiah 43:19).

"But if the LORD creates something new … then you shall know that these men have despised the LORD" (Numbers 16:30).

Before my next chapter resolves the Korah story, let's put ourselves in Moses' shoes. Most of us could cite good reasons to decline this time-machine journey. "We are needed here, especially by family." "Nobody in the company knows how to do my job." "My doctor has advised me not to travel." "Desert sand and wind would stir up my allergies."

Would our reason justify an excused absence? Or would it be just an excuse? Many would not want to be in Moses's sandals, because they stepped out on a limb that would break unless God came through for him. Henry Blackaby, in *Experiencing God*, calls this a crisis of belief. We believe in theory that God can heal, but for the sick people we love or have been asked to pray for, we don't think that He will. God can still work miracles today, but usually does not. And if the miracle we need would require suspending the natural laws of geophysics, forget it. But as Blackaby warns, "You can't stay where you are, and go with God."

How long since there has been anything significantly new in your spiritual life, church, or denomination? Many could paraphrase Jesus' parable about new wine, found in all three of the synoptic gospels. Here's the Luke 5:37–39 version, which adds a zinger at the end:

> *"And no one puts new wine into old wineskins. If he does, the new wine will burst the skins and it will be spilled, and the skins will be destroyed. But new wine must be put into fresh wineskins. And no one after drinking old wine desires new, for he says, 'The old is good.'"*

Moses was the opposite. He was used to the new because he had so much of it. Moses' whole life was out of the box. He was pulled from a boat box soon after his birth. He was never put in a burial box at his death. In contrast to contemporary Christians whose religious rituals remain routine and whose theological ideas traveled intact from their ancestors, God's mantra for Moses was "new." Scripture notes at least thirty-two of his experiences which were firsts for the human race.

As far as we know, Moses was the only person who experienced the following:

- had parents who launched him into a river rife with hungry crocodiles
- was saved by Egyptians during their pogrom to eliminate Hebrews
- had a mother whom a hostile regime paid to raise her son
- was a Jewish boy with a legitimate chance to become pharaoh
- experienced life in three contrasting periods of forty years each

- had God speak to him through a burning bush
- turned water into blood and then back into water
- possessed a staff-turned-snake that swallowed other staffs-turned-snakes
- proliferated frogs instantaneously and then made them die, except those he exempted
- turned dust into gnats
- parted the Red Sea
- spent forty days with God on Mount Sinai twice

Moses was the only person to ever experience the things listed above. Each of these was a new thing when it happened. Moses was also the first person to have the experiences below. As each of these materialized, it was a new thing. Moses was not the first Jew to be sent as a missionary (Abram was) or to be mistaken for an Egyptian (Joseph beat him to this). Moses was the first to experience the following:

- live as a Hebrew in Midian after living in Egypt
- have God reveal Himself as "I Am Who I Am"
- have God tell him to go barefooted
- stand on holy ground
- be commissioned to assemble Israel's elders
- get leprosy and be healed
- receive a threat from God to kill his firstborn son
- have a spokeman whom God assigned
- claim a speech impediment
- receive a magic staff
- cause Hebrews in Egypt to worship
- ask God why
- hear God call Israel His firstborn

- produce swarms of flies and dictate where they could and could not go and when they left
- produce a plague that killed Egyptian livestock but spared Hebrew livestock
- turn inanimate soot into animate boils
- send Egypt's worst killer hailstorm ever and then remove it in a moment
- send enough locusts to cover Egypt and kill all plant life and then send them into the Red Sea
- send three days of total darkness on Egypt but spare Goshen

Korah's crew caught Moses off guard when they confronted him and Aaron the day before. He was shocked speechless and fell limp in prostrate prayer. Words failed him, not just to his caustic critics but to his loving Lord. He could only groan, but our groan will reach God's throne. It was his people's groan which had gotten Moses involved in this in the first place when he was in Midian minding his own business.

And the people of Israel groaned because of their slavery and cried out for help. Their cry for rescue from slavery came up to God. And God heard their groaning, and God remembered his covenant with Abraham, with Isaac, and with Jacob. God saw the people of Israel — and God knew (Exodus 2:23–25).

Now Moses was keeping the flock of his father-in-law, Jethro ... and he led his flock to the west side of the wilderness and came to Horeb, the mountain of God. ... When the LORD saw that he turned aside to see, God called to him out of the [burning] bush, "Moses, Moses!" ... Then the LORD said, "I have surely seen the affliction of my people who are in Egypt and have heard their cry because of their taskmasters. I know their sufferings, and I have come down to deliver them … . And now, behold, the cry of the people of Israel has come to me … . Come, I will send you to Pharaoh that you may bring my people, the children of Israel, out of Egypt" (Exodus 3:1, 4, 7–10).

God heard the groaning of His people and sent Moses to deliver them. God heard Moses' groaning at the showdown at sunset. Because our groan reaches God's throne, He will answer the call to deliver even if it means God doing something new from our viewpoint. The Holy Spirit showed me that, from God's perspective, Korah's earthquake was the same basic miracle the Lord did at the Red Sea — but that one was with water, while this one was with dirt. Since our bodies are from the dust of the earth and hold a lot of water, God does not need a new category of miracles to work in our behalf!

CHAPTER 12

SOMETHING NEW: KORAH, DATHAN, AND ABIRAM

And Moses said, "Hereby you shall know that the LORD has sent me to do all these works, and that it has not been of my own accord. If these men die as all men die, or if they are visited by the fate of all mankind, then the LORD has not sent me. But if the LORD creates something new, and the ground opens its mouth and swallows them up with all that belongs to them, and they go down alive into Sheol, then you shall know that these men have despised the LORD" (Numbers 16:28–30).

On February 6, 2023, a 7.8 magnitude earthquake struck south and central Turkey and north and western Syria, killing 55,700 and injuring 130,000. Its magnitude and deadliness were exceeded only by earthquakes in 1268 and 1668 in Turkey and by a Syrian earthquake in 1822. The 2023 quake was felt from the Black Sea coast to Cyprus, Lebanon, Israel, Palestine, and Egypt.

Because Egypt was such a world power in the second millennium BC, Moses' geography and science classes in Egypt's palace would have at least mentioned this earthquake zone that included them. Earthquakes and other natural disasters are often classified as acts of God. It is obvious from Moses' description above that an earthquake was the natural phenomenon God would use to take out the chief conspirators. But it would require supernatural shaping to take out only the ringleaders and to neatly reclose the earth's surface once they were gone. Moses knew the plan by this point. This was an advance illustration of Amos 3:7–8:

> "For the Lord GOD does nothing without revealing his secret to his servants the prophets. The lion has roared; who will not fear? The Lord GOD has spoken; who can but prophesy?"

Moses had exhibited a peace from the start of this crisis. His very first words in response to Korah's attack were "In the morning the LORD will show …" (Numbers 16:5). He trusted God to take care of this, even before he knew exactly how the Lord would do so. New Testament believers have a much greater body of evidence for God's faithfulness for us and through the example of others:

> The Lord is at hand; do not be anxious about anything, but in everything by prayer and supplication with thanksgiving let your requests be made known to God. And the peace of God, which surpasses all understanding, will guard your hearts and your minds in Christ Jesus. … What you have learned and received and heard and seen in me — practice these things, and the God of peace will be with you (Philippians 4:5b–7, 9).

Moses was right. The Lord did show. First, the Lord showed up the next morning once the human actors in this drama were in place. "And the glory of the LORD appeared to all the congregation." This was probably the "shekinah glory" cloud through which God would manifest His presence and from which God would speak. God's mind is made up. He comes not for a discussion but for a disposition.

"And the LORD spoke to Moses and to Aaron, saying, 'Separate yourselves from among this congregation, that I may consume them in a moment'" (Numbers 16:20-21). Moses and Aaron pleaded for God to punish just Korah and let the others off. But God's first verdict gave Dathan and Abiram the same sentence as Korah: "And the LORD spoke to Moses, saying, 'Say to the congregation, Get away from the dwelling of Korah, Dathan, and Abiram'" (Numbers 16:23–24).

Because Dathan and Abiram were still at home from when they slipped out the day before, Moses made a house call, and the crowd followed him. But Moses was done talking with them, so he warned the innocent bystanders to get out of the way:

> *"Quick!" he told the people. "Get away from the tents if these wicked men, and don't touch anything that belongs to them. If you do, you will be destroyed for their sins." So all the people stood back from the tents of Korah, Dathan, and Abiram (Numbers 16:26-27a, NLT).*

This illustrates the way of escape from temptation that God offers believers today:

> *Now these things happened to them as an example, but they were written down for our instruction, on whom the end of the ages has come. Therefore let anyone who thinks that he stands take heed lest he fall. No temptation has overtaken you that is not common to man. God is faithful, and he will not let you be tempted beyond your ability, but with the temptation will also provide the way of escape, that you may be able to endure it (1 Corinthians 10:11–13).*

"And Dathan and Abiram came out and stood at the door of their tents, together with their wives, their sons, and their little ones" (Numbers 16:27b). The sheepish, silent reaction of these two families hints that their heads of household were simple, naïve men who underestimated the weight of their actions. Too slowly, they realized how deeply they were getting in, and what it would cost their families.

Lines had been drawn in the sand. After the people had chosen how they would line up, Moses stressed that this was a test case. Had God really called and authorized Moses to lead? Or had Moses taken it upon himself to be in charge? Moses throws down the gauntlet:

> And Moses said, "Hereby you shall know that the LORD has sent me to do all these works, and that it has not been of my own accord. If these men die as all men die, or if they are visited by the fate of all mankind, then the LORD has not sent me. But if the LORD creates something new, and the ground opens its mouth and swallows them … and they go down alive into Sheol, then you shall know that these men have despised the LORD" (Numbers 16:28–30).

Korah, Dathan, and Abiram had long despised Moses. But since God had made him the leader, to despise Moses as leader was to also despise God. If God had struck these men with a fatal heart attack or cerebral hemorrhage on the spot, rational people would have agreed it was God's judgment. But Moses (and God) wanted to leave no doubt about it. It would be not just a new and unique manner of capital punishment, but Moses spelled out in advance exactly what would take them off the earth.

It was obvious that these three were going down and would physically vacate the earth. Moses called their new abode *Sheol* — which the Hebrew Bible mentions sixty-six times as the place of the dead. Some Bible translations nickname this the pit, a literal description of its depth, despair, and desperation. *Sheol* itself was not new, for it appears in Genesis 37:35, 44:29–31, but Korah, Dathan, and Abiram were going there in a new way.

> *And as soon as he had finished speaking all these words, the ground under them split apart. And the earth opened its mouth and swallowed them up, with their households and all the people who belonged to Korah and all their goods. So they and all that belonged to them went down alive into Sheol, and the earth closed over them, and they perished from the midst of the assembly. And all Israel who were around them fled at their cry, for they said, "Lest the earth swallow us up!" (Numbers 16:31–34).*

This occurrence was obviously not photographed. In all of my research into Jewish history, I have seen only one artistic impression of how it may have looked. As you glance at this book's cover, notice that the artist has rendered the split-second that Korah's company was below ground level before the earth closed over them. Their tents are the large, yellow objects. It is a horrifying picture. Too late, they realized the severity of what they had said and done and the finality of their fate.

Colonial America used *The New England Primer* to teach children to read. They first had to learn the alphabet, which had an object for each letter with a brief statement. Korah represents "K" in the 1768 edition, which states, "Proud Korah's troop was swallowed up."

CHAPTER 13

CENSURED: KORAH'S 250 CHIEFS

"And fire came out from the LORD and consumed the 250 men offering the incense" (Numbers 16:35).

T he last verse on the day before, and the first verse on showdown day concerned the censers:

"And let every one of you take his censer and put incense on it, and every one of you bring before the LORD his censer, 250 censers; you also, and Aaron, each his censer" (Numbers 16:17).

So every man took his censer and put fire in them and laid incense on them and stood at the entrance of the tent of meeting with Moses and Aaron (Numbers 16:18).

What was a censer? It comes from the word incense and was used to burn incense in the tabernacle:

"The vessel in which incense was presented on the golden (incense) altar before the Lord in the temple (or tabernacle, in the outer room called the holy place), (Exodus 30:1–9). The priest filled the censer with live coals from the sacred fire on the altar of burnt offering, and having carried them into the sanctuary, there threw on the burning coals the sweet incense, which sent up a cloud of smoke filling the room with fragrance (Leviticus 16:12–13).

> And he shall take a censer full of coals of fire from the altar before the Lord, and two handfuls of sweet incense beaten small, and he shall bring it inside the veil and put the incense on the fire before the Lord, that the cloud of the incense may cover the mercy seat that is over the testimony [the ark of the covenant], so that he does not die.
>
> The censers in daily use were "brass."
>
> *(M.G. Easton, "Censer," Easton's Bible Dictionary)*

Censers in biblical times were made of gold or bronze. The gold censers in Exodus 25:38 and Leviticus were in the Holy Place and used by the priests with the altar of incense. These very limited editions were made by Bezaleel himself. The censers in 1 Kings 7:50 and 2 Chronicles 4:22 were gold, but these were in the Temple, centuries later.

Most of the censers in the wilderness period were bronze or brass, both of which symbolized judgment. This metal is called brass in older Bible translations and bronze in newer ones. Its Hebrew word *nehosheth* covers multiple copper alloys.

Censers had two main uses in the wilderness: ceremonial or practical. Fires were used for light, warmth, and cooking, so each tent needed a firepan. The outer court of the tabernacle also needed censers for the priests and Levites to use at the bronze or brazen altar, in conjunction with the animal sacrifices for sin.

Korah was revolting against an exclusive priesthood of just Aaron and his sons and their direct descendants. He wanted the priesthood to be expanded to include any Hebrew adult males wanting to serve in this capacity. As his revolt played out, the irony was that there were only enough of the sacred censers for the Aaronic priests. When 250 men showed up wanting the priesthood, they had to bring their residential censers, which God would quickly and automatically disqualify as being profane, not sacred. The mere mention of these common censers upped the ante, heralding the high stakes of the showdown at sunrise.

"And fire came out from the LORD and consumed the 250 men offering the incense" (Numbers 16:35).

Inside the tabernacle, censers were to bring a sweet smell before the Lord. But outside the tabernacle at this showdown, these residential censers stank before the Lord. God dismissed out of hand the idea that the priesthood could be widened and watered down to include any man who wanted to be a priest.

Then the LORD spoke to Moses, saying, "Tell Eleazar the son of Aaron the priest to take up the censers out of the blaze. Then scatter the fire far and wide, for they have become holy. As for the censers of these men who have sinned at the cost of their lives, let them be made into hammered plates as a covering for the altar, for they offered them before the LORD, and they became holy. Thus they shall be a sign to the people of Israel" (Numbers 16:36–38).

It is interesting that God gave this crisis assignment not to Aaron but to his son Eleazer. God may have seen this as a strenuous task, which would have taxed the eighty-five-year-old Aaron. I believe it was to make a statement. Korah and his crew wanted the priesthood to be expanded. God was vetoing a horizontal expansion which would have taken it outside Aaron's branch of the family tree. God was satisfied with his original intent to expand it vertically down Aaron's lineage.

So Eleazar the priest took the bronze censers, which those who were burned had offered, and they were hammered out as a covering for the altar, to be a reminder to the people of Israel, so that no outsider, who is not of the descendants of Aaron, should draw near to burn incense before the LORD, lest he become like Korah and his company — as the LORD said to him through Moses (Numbers 16:39–40).

Today, we would have rounded up these censers and put them in a dumpster or hauled them to a scrap metal site. But God said the censers had become holy, although the hands that held them were not. It was their having been offered to the Lord that made them holy.

Grumbling followed:

But on the next day all the congregation of the people of Israel grumbled against Moses and against Aaron, saying, "You have killed the people of the LORD" (Numbers 16:41).

The rank-and-file saw the physical, not the spiritual. The New Testament explanation is in 1 Corinthians 2:14: "The natural person does not accept the things of the Spirit of God, for they are folly to him, and he is not able to understand them because they are spiritually discerned."

And when the congregation had assembled against Moses and against Aaron, they turned toward the tent of meeting. And behold, the cloud covered it, and the glory of the LORD appeared. And Moses and Aaron came to the front of the tent of meeting, and the LORD spoke to Moses, saying, "Get away from the midst of this congregation, that I may consume them in a moment."

And they fell on their faces (Numbers 16:42–45).

God demonstrated once again that to challenge or reject His divinely appointed people, principles, or procedures is to attack Him. He takes it personally.

And Moses said to Aaron, "Take your censer, and put fire on it from off the altar and lay incense on it and carry it quickly to the congregation and make atonement for them, for wrath has gone out from the LORD; the plague has begun" (Numbers 16:46).

Eleazar may be worn out from, or still carrying out his prior assignment. Aaron has largely been just a silent witness to the morning's happenings, so Moses gives him an assignment, to put him back in action. A priest is a mediator who goes between God and the people. Aaron would do this now.

So Aaron took it as Moses said and ran into the midst of the assembly. And behold, the plague had already begun among the people. And he put on the incense and made atonement for the people. And he stood between the dead and the living, and the plague was stopped (Numbers 16:47–48).

As believers today in a society where most are not, we stand between the spiritually dead and the spiritually alive. Most Americans think they will go to heaven when they die, but Jesus says in Matthew 7:13–14 that most will not: "Enter by the narrow gate. For the gate is wide and the way is easy that leads to destruction, and those who enter by it are many. For the gate is narrow and the way is hard that leads to life, and those who find it are few." The gate to salvation on earth and eternity in heaven is narrow because Jesus is the only way. He says in John 14:6, "I am the way, and the truth, and the life. No one comes to the Father except through me."

The plague killed 14,700 people, and the 250 leaders were killed by the fire of God's judgment.

> *Now those who died in the plague were 14,700, besides those who died in the affair of Korah. And Aaron returned to Moses at the entrance of the tent of meeting, when the plague was stopped (Numbers 16:49–50).*

Except for Assir, Elkanah and Abiasaph, the families of Korah, Dathan, and Abiram plunged to their death when the earth swallowed their tents. So about fifteen thousand people died that day, casualties of Korah's rebellion. Would they have lived to see another day had Korah kept his mouth shut?

> *Your hand will find out all your enemies; your right hand will find out those who hate you. You will make them as a blazing oven when you appear. The LORD will swallow them up in his wrath, and fire will consume them. … Though they plan evil against you, though they devise mischief, they will not succeed (Psalm 21:8–9, 11).*

CHAPTER 14

VICTIMIZED: SONS OF KORAH

Why has the LORD brought us to this land to fall by the sword, that our wives and children should become victims? (Numbers 14:3, NKJV).

But your little ones, whom you said would be victims, I will bring in, and they shall know the land which you have despised (Numbers 14:31, NKJV).

These are the Dathan and Abiram, chosen from the congregation, who contended against Moses and Aaron in the company of Korah, when they contended against the LORD and the earth opened its mouth and swallowed them up together with Korah, when that company died, when the fire devoured 250 men, and they became a warning. But the sons of Korah did not die (Numbers 26:9b–11).

Armed conflicts, natural disasters, and "acts of God" lead to casualties. They create two types of victims. Dathan, Abiram, and Korah were victims of God's response to their rebellion. Assir, Elkanah, and Abiasaph, the sons of Korah, were victimized by their father's rebellion.

The lives of Assir, Elkanah, and Abiasaph would be forever changed by Korah's conflict. The only question was whether they would be victims in it or victimized by it. Had they just floated with the tide, the current would have swept them away.

Korah's resentment of Moses and Aaron seems to have been sour grapes that they were given a position Korah coveted for himself. In and around their family tent, his sons probably overheard their share of his rants against their uncles. Although their father may have blown this out of proportion, Korah's teen boys guessed there may be a grain of truth in his gripes. They had hoped to stay out of this family feud. But an early morning shout from Uncle Moses took away the tiny middle ground they had clung to: "Quick!" he told the people. "Get away from the tents of these wicked men, and don't touch anything that belongs to them. If you do, you will be destroyed for their sins" (Numbers 16:26, NLT).

These may have been the last words Korah's sons heard before their world fell apart … literally. If Moses was just bluffing, and they stepped away from their tent, they would be *persona non grata* the rest of their parents' lives. But, if this was a warning from the Lord, that Moses was just delivering, they could be swept away. The family feud had gotten ugly. They had tried to stay out of this adult argument, which had reached epic proportions at yesterday's faceoff.

It *May* Have Happened Like This

If it ever came to taking sides, the boys would have wanted some time to discuss it among themselves so they could stick together in their decision. But Uncle Moses' words and tone had lit the fuse. Time was ticking away, quickly.

They stared at each other. Assir pointed away from the tent. Elkanah and Abiasaph were reluctant, gently shaking their heads to decline. Assir whispered, "It's now or never." Their mouths gaped in stunned silence. But when they did not say "no," Assir stepped between his younger brothers, grabbed each one by an upper arm, and ran from the tent. This way, they did not have to make eye contact with their parents. They were also spared from seeing how it would go down, although the sound was deafening.

The burst, the thrust, their emotions, and their spent energy flung them to the ground. Shrieks of horror cascaded and echoed around the camp. But not a word was heard for what seemed like an eternity. Then they detected in the distance a voice everyone recognized. It was Moses. In his urgent attempt to see the whole scene at once, he had not been able to focus on individuals who may have stepped away from the tents targeted. But his three frantic words said it all: "Assir? Elkanah? Abiathar?"

A rabbinic tradition has it that the sons of Korah were profoundly influenced by the goodness of Moses. In spite of the negative propaganda spread by Korah's group, his sons realized that Moses was a humble man, not at all desirous of power over others. He was a leader not by his personal choice or inclination, but because God laid the responsibilities upon him. Moses lived simply; he did not use his position to become wealthy or for any personal gain. He did not lord it over the people, but indeed was their humble servant and advocate. The sons of Korah were able to see through the falsehoods spread by the rebels. They had the strength of character to stand with Moses against the wicked designs of Korah. *(Rabbi Marc D. Angel, www.jewishideas.org/ sons-korah-and-us-thoughts-parashot-korah)*

Korah's sons' desperate decision saved their lives. But they lost everything else! Starting with the most immediate and obvious, we can count on the fingers of one hand the categories of what they lost. Their right choice cost them their rights to their parents, their home, possessions, companions, and good name. They would be victimized long and hard because what they had loved and depended on the most had been snatched away.

Although the loss of a child by parents is the greatest grief, the sudden loss of both **parents** by minor children is the greatest trauma. Their world is turned upside down. All the certainties they have taken for granted during their whole lives have vanished to be replaced by waves of worries, questions, and unknowns.

A month ago, the sons of Korah would have looked forward to entering the Promised Land with their parents — coming of age there, building houses next to their parents, and raising grandchildren for them in a land flowing with milk and honey. But the milk had soured, and the honey pot had crashed on the hard ground. Father had grown distant in recent days, but Mother had remained the one who cared for them and met their every need. They would miss her sweet smile whenever she glanced at them and her warm hugs when they got hurt physically or emotionally. They still had a decade before they could carry the sacred articles in the tabernacle whenever the cloud moved, and this holy tent went with it. But their father had always talked about when they would do this and given tips of the trade to them.

Their **home** had disappeared. They were glad they were looking the other way when this happened. But what would they do now? Where would they live? Their big tent beat that tiny hut in Egypt. Although they had moved around in the wilderness, the tent they loved and lived in was always the same. Father had taught them how to take it down, transport it, and put it back up while he was moving the things in the holy tent. Their parents slept on one side of the tent, and they had their three spots on the other side.

They did not have many **possessions** besides the clothes on their back and the sandals on their feet. But they treasured the few things they could call their own. Their five bowls and cups may have looked the same to strangers, but the family knew which was whose. Extra utensils were rare around the camp, so what would they eat from now? And where would they eat? It had not dawned on them when they left their tent that this might be a moving day.

Their loss of **companions** beyond their parents would not have occurred to us, but they wrote of it. "You have caused my companions to shun me; you have made me a horror to them" (Psalm 88:8); "I am helpless" (88:15); and "You have caused my beloved and my friend to shun me; my companions have become darkness" (88:18).

Because the 250 tribal chiefs in Korah's company were incinerated by God's judgment fire, all the survivors in the camp would have lost some leaders. They would have blamed this on Korah and may have taken it out on his sons. Most of the Hebrews would be grieving and griping about friends, neighbors, and close relatives in the 14,700 who died in the plague that followed. Only Korah's sons were left as a target at which they could vent their accusations and lamentations.

Last but not least, Korah's sons lost their **good name**. Korah is in the vilest of the Bible's villains. He is one of only three Old Testament characters named and vilified as bad examples in the last New Testament book before Revelation (Jude 11). How would you like to be known the rest of your life and in history's millennia since as "the sons of Korah"?

Many know this phrase and its guilt by association, but few could even differentiate them by their given names. A Bible verse they love now is Revelation 2:17, where the risen and reigning Christ promises:

"To the one who conquers I will give some of the hidden manna, and I will give him a white stone, with a new name written on the stone that no one knows except the one who receives it" *(Revelation 2:17).*

Would-be victims can be victors! The sons of Korah were.

VICTIMIZED

Bottomed Out

In which of the following ways have you been victimized?

- Loved ones died or moved away
- Health issues, handicaps, debilitating illnesses, serious injuries
- Divorce, separation, broken or strained relationships
- Abuse (physical, sexual, verbal, financial)
- Addictions (gambling, alcohol, drugs, pornography)
- Bullying, crime, scams, identity theft
- Job loss, demotion, hard boss, crass co-workers
- Financial loss, home or vehicle repossessed, bankruptcy
- Traffic accident, fire, natural disaster
- Lawsuits, taken to court, incarcerated, institutionalized
- Malice, slander, rumors, gossip, social media

What are the lingering effects from the above?

Battling Back

To move from victim to victor, try the following:

- Do not point your finger at the Lord in criticism or blame
- Do pour out your heart to the Lord for comfort and blessing

In Psalm 88, the sons of Korah were still suffering the horrors of Korah's judgment. You can feel their pain and hear their cries as they pour out their anguish to the Lord. This psalm is a great example and pattern of how to pour out your hurt to our heavenly Father.

Your first step should be a decisive moment. Their *carpe diem* was to obey Moses' desperate plea: "Get away from the tents of these wicked men!" (Numbers 16:26, NLT).

"I would rather be a doorkeeper in the house of my God than dwell in the tents of wickedness" (Psalm 84:10).

Is there something you should step away from to start your recovery process? What is the decisive step you can take to move from victim to becoming a victor? To move from victim to victor, stand for the Lord no matter who is against you — no matter if it is:

- the people (Korah gathered all the congregation against them, Numbers 16:9).
- the powerful (250 chiefs, famous in the congregation, men of renown, Numbers 16:2), or
- their patriarch (their father Korah's rebellion, Jude 11).

The sons of Korah were Levites. A whole Bible book before the Levites were commissioned and consecrated to be God's special tribe, there was a crisis moment after the golden calf idolatry and its ensuing immorality where God's leader needed help to change the congregational direction:

And when Moses saw that the people had broken loose (for Aaron had let them break loose, to the derision of their enemies), then Moses stood in the gate of the camp and said, "Who is on the Lord's side? Come to me." And all the sons of Levi gathered around him. And he said to them, "Thus says the Lord God of Israel, 'Put your sword on your side each of you, and go to and fro from gate to gate throughout the camp, and each of you kill his brother and his companion and his neighbor.'" And the sons of Levi did according to the word of Moses. And that day about three thousand men of the people fell. And Moses said, "Today

*you have been ordained for the service of the LORD, each one
at the cost of his son and of his brother, so that he (God) might
bestow a blessing upon you this day" (Exodus 32:25-29).*

Thank goodness that under the New Testament covenant of grace,
God does not ask believers to execute sinners in the name of the Lord
but to obey and put Him first. There are times when we must go against
the advice and counsel of our friends, neighbors, loved ones, super-
visors, or church members.

"To illustrate the point, Jesus compared love for Him with
love for family (Luke 14:26–27). The depth of my love for Jesus
may make my love for anyone or anything else look like hate.
At times, my love for Jesus may lead to tension or distance from
my relationships with people who are not intent on following
Jesus. *(Seven Arrows Bible, 2019, Nashville, TN: Holman Bible
Publishers, p. 1078)*

Victors stay with the Lord
- No matter how bad it gets, their groanings in Psalm 88 show
  how deep was their pain.
- No matter how long it takes.

Levites served age thirty to fifty — twenty years of active duty, like
our military careers. The sons of Korah added ten-plus years on the
front end, starting in their teens.

*Shallum the son of Kore, son of Ebiasaph, son of Korah, and his
kinsmen of his fathers' house, the Korahites, were in charge of the
work of the service, keepers of the thresholds of the tent, as their*

fathers had been in charge of the camp of the LORD, *keepers of the entrance (1 Chronicles 9:19).*

Victors speak for the Lord

The sons of Korah praised God for their victories:

- *"Why are you cast down, O my soul, and why are you in turmoil within me?" (Psalm 42:5).*
- *"Why are you cast down, O my soul, and why are you in turmoil within me? Hope in God; for I shall again praise him, my salvation and my God" (Psalm 42:11).*
- *"In God we have boasted continually, and we will give thanks to your name forever" (Psalm 44:8).*
- *"God is our refuge and strength, a very present help in trouble. Therefore we will not fear though the earth gives way" (Psalm 46:1–2a).*
- *"For God is the King of all the earth; sing praises with a psalm!" (Psalm 47:7).*

They also pointed others to God for their victories:

- *"Blessed are those whose strength is in you, in whose heart are the highways to Zion" (Psalm 84:5).*
- *"As they go through the Valley of Baca (weeping) they make it a place of springs" (Psalm 84:6).*

As we pass through the valley of weeping as victims but victors in the Lord, our tears become a well of living water to nurture the hopes and dreams of other victims, so they, too, may become victors in the Lord.

Be victorious through the Lord

- *"But thanks be to God, who gives us the victory through our Lord Jesus Christ" (1 Corinthians 15:57).*
- *"And this is the victory that has overcome the world — our faith" (1 John 5:4b).*
- *"In all these things we are more than conquerors through him who loved us" (Romans 8:37).*

CHAPTER 15

JOINT CHIEFS?

And the LORD spake unto Moses, saying, "Speak unto the children of Israel, and take of every one of them a rod according to the house of their fathers, of all their princes according to the house of their fathers, twelve rods: write thou every man's name upon his rod. And thou shalt write Aaron's name upon the rod of Levi: for one rod shall be for the head of the house of their fathers. And thou shalt lay them up in the tabernacle of the congregation before the testimony, where I will meet with you. And it shall come to pass, that the man's rod, whom I shall choose, shall blossom: and I will make to cease from me the murmurings of the children of Israel, whereby they murmur against you. And Moses spake unto the children of Israel, and every one of their princes gave him a rod apiece, for each prince one, according to their fathers' houses, even twelve rods: and the rod of Aaron was among their rods. And Moses laid up the rods before the LORD in the tabernacle of witness (Numbers 17:1–7, KJV).

Remember that Korah challenged the singularity of the Aaronic priesthood, believing it should be opened up to himself and others who may desire it. Although Korah was gone, God sensed that sentiment could resurface. So he initiates another object lesson to underscore that singular leadership was his idea and his will. God did not want joint chiefs in the spiritual or governmental realms of his people Israel. God reaffirms here that He will continue to relate with and work through His one appointed and anointed leader in each realm.

This chapter's Scripture text above is from the King James Version for the best translation of its key words: rod instead of staff, princes instead of chiefs, and children instead of people. Although KJV wording sounds archaic today, its rendering of these key words seems truer to the Hebrew they translate. These words much better fit the context of this chapter and God's purpose in this demonstration.

The Lord as David's shepherd comforted him in Psalm 23:4 with His rod and staff. Which shepherd's tool is the subject in Numbers chapter 17? Today's best-selling Bible translations choose staff here, but its context and Hebrew vocabulary suggest rod. A Christian classic for over a half-century is *A Shepherd Looks at Psalm 23*. Phillip Keller, a shepherd himself, first published this book in 1970. He writes, "The rod is what he relied on to safeguard both himself and his flock in danger. It was the instrument he used to discipline and correct any wayward sheep. The rod's most frequent use was for discipline."

The main Hebrew word for rod is *matteh*, "a rod," used in the Old Testament forty-four times. Three-fourths of the occurrences are by Moses, including ten in this chapter. Almost half of Moses' uses are in Exodus, where his rod was God-empowered (Exodus 4:20). This rod swallowed the serpent-rods of Pharaoh's magicians, brought the plagues on Egypt, parted the Red Sea, and won victory over Amalek. What God planned in Numbers chapter 17 was not caring for his flock with a staff, but their correcting with a rod.

This is the first action the Bible records after the showdown day with Korah, Dathan, and Abiram. It was God's initiative. Moses and Aaron probably thought that yesterday's events forever established the legitimacy and authority of the Aaronic priesthood once and for all. But

God knew we have short memories. So, He initiated another episode. God had said multiple times that Aaron was the High Priest, but this event would pair with chapter 16 as the two witnesses to show it.

In the book of Numbers, what leaders are called can be ambiguous. The main Hebrew word *nasi* is translated "chief" or "prince," but the adjective "twelve" here specifies the leader of each of the twelve tribes. The 250 chiefs who joined Korah's rebellion were obviously not the chiefs of their own tribes, so prince better fits the context here. The dozen tribe-level leaders are the subjects of interest in the text printed above. They are not named again here, as they have already been named as their tribal chiefs twice in Numbers (2:3–29 and 7:12–78). The absence of names here implies that there have been no changes in this roster. Your writer infers this to also be God's signal that they are not as important as they think they are.

"The rod of Aaron was among their rods" (v. 6) could be interpreted as "twelve plus Aaron's." Thirteen is the Bible's number to symbolize rebellion. But "write Aaron's name on the staff of Levi" implies his among the twelve (v. 3). What Moses recorded God as saying seems to hark back to the original twelve sons of Jacob, named three times in Genesis and including Levi's name each time (29:34, 46:11, 49:5).

This makes "children of Israel" (17:1, 5, 6, 9, 12) a better translation than "people of Israel." The Hebrew word is ben, meaning "son" or "produce." It also fits the context, as they had been immature in their actions. Although the 253 ringleaders had paid with their deaths, they had sympathizers left in the camp.

This demonstration will be God's doing, so He gives Moses specific instructions, which are clear to the twelve princes or chiefs. They provided their own rods, which they would recognize afterward. Moses writes each prince's name on the prince's rod, obviously with the prince watching closely. These sticks would spend the night with God in the tabernacle. The English Standard Version reads, "And Moses deposited" them. This made the tabernacle a night depository this once, and the dozen rods would be withdrawn with interest the next morning. Aaron's rod was the only rod with interest on it. The other rods had interest in them, by the princes who owned them plus any Israelite still wanting a plurality of leadership. God declared in advance that He will authenticate only one of them by causing it to sprout.

> On the next day Moses went into the tent of the testimony, and behold, the staff of Aaron for the house of Levi had sprouted and put forth buds and produced blossoms, and it bore ripe almonds. Then Moses brought out all the staffs from before the Lord to all the people of Israel. And they looked, and each man took his staff (Numbers 17:8–9).

With all twelve candidates on hand the next morning, Moses retrieved all the staffs. He brought them to the group. Each man took his staff, with his name on it to verify that it is indeed his. Eleven rods were as dead as they were the day before. Aaron's rod was very alive, with three stages of growth. God showed up and showed out. The Apostle Paul exhorts us to picture a big God who can do great things: "Now to him who is able to do far more abundantly than all that we ask or think, according to the power at work within us, to him be glory in the church and in Christ Jesus throughout all generations, forever and ever. Amen" (Ephesians 3:20–21).

> And the Lord said unto Moses, "Bring Aaron's rod again before the testimony, to be kept for a token against the rebels; and thou shalt quite take away their murmurings from me, that they die not." And Moses did so: as the Lord commanded him, so did he.

And the children of Israel spake unto Moses, saying, "Behold, we die, we perish, we all perish. Whosoever cometh any thing near unto the tabernacle of the LORD shall die: shall we be consumed with dying?" (Numbers 17:10–13, KJV).

It appears that there were some rebels left, even after yesterday's earthquake, fire, and plague.

God hears our grumbling, and he hates and detests it. As New Testament believers, our grumbling says that we are dissatisfied with our heavenly Father's provision for us. We should memorize and meditate on 1 Timothy 6:6: "Godliness with contentment is great gain."

It is common knowledge that the Hebrews' refusal to enter Canaan immediately was the occasion for God's sentence that none of them age twenty and up besides Caleb and Joshua would enter the Promised Land. Few realize that it was their grumbling that pushed God to make this decree (Numbers 14:26–32). The rest of them would die off in the wilderness during the next four decades — "But the sons of Korah did not die" (Numbers 26:11). From this we can deduce that the sons of Korah were still teenagers when their father rebelled.

Korah's company showed that 250 chiefs did not want a chief over them. They had wanted to be joint chiefs. They were gone now in the fatal flames. But God did not want their successors to pick up this ball and run with it. The twelve princes this day would each relay the message back to his tribe.

All the way toward the end of the New Testament, Hebrews 9:3–4 (KJV) mentions this object of remembrance:

And after the second veil, the tabernacle which is called the Holiest of all; which had the golden censer, and the ark of the covenant overlaid round about with gold, wherein was the golden pot that had manna, and Aaron's rod that budded, and the tables of the covenant.

This detail adds a third reason (the first being Hebrew vocabulary; the second, the context) that God was talking about rods, not staffs. A rod was a short, heavy club. A staff was a long stick, often with a shepherd's crook at the end to help the shepherd safely lift a fallen sheep out of a pit or ravine. Google *Experiencing God*. On the revised and expanded Bible study, notice the artist's cover drawing of Moses (the study's focal character). He is pictured with staff in hand. A shepherd typically leaned on his staff, which rested on solid ground. Notice that Moses' staff is taller than he is. As brothers, Moses and Aaron likely were of similar heights. Since a staff was customized to one's height, fitting Aaron's staff into the ark of the covenant would have required a short Aaron.

According to Exodus 25:10 and 37:1, this ark was 2.5 cubits long by 1.5 cubits wide and 1.5 cubits high. A cubit was the length of a man's bent forearm from the tip of the elbow to the fingertips. The biblical cubit was estimated at eighteen inches, the exact measurement of this 5'8" author's cubit. The ark was about forty-five inches long, so a four-foot staff would not fit without using the ark's diagonal interior, which also contained the stone tablets engraved with the Ten Commandments and a pot of manna.

For an informative, detailed sermon outline on Aaron's rod that budded, read: David Guzik, © 2022, *The Enduring Word Commentary* https://enduringword.com/bible-commentary/numbers-17.

CHAPTER 16

FROM VICTIMS TO VICTORS: SONS OF KORAH

The Hebrews who were left in the wilderness still had quantity — almost two million people. But their quality had tanked in many ways.

First, they had all left Egyptian slavery a year ago for the promise of freedom in a land flowing with milk and honey. This wilderness was anything but that. They had been eating mainly manna every day for a year, and there was often no fresh water, much less any flowing milk.

Second, all but two of the adults had received a divine sentence to die in this wilderness.

Third, about fifteen-thousand Hebrews had just been executed by God for rebelling against His delegated leaders for government and religion.

Fourth, some felt God had piled on and rubbed salt into the wound by doing an overnight miracle just to underscore the authority of His appointed religious leader.

Finally, because the recent rebellion attacked the pinnacle of the leadership pyramid, God will tighten security at the entrance to the tabernacle, which served as their massive town square.

So the LORD said to Aaron, "You and your sons and your father's house with you shall bear iniquity connected with the sanctuary, and you and your sons with you shall bear iniquity connected with your priesthood. And with you bring your brothers also, the tribe of Levi, the tribe of your father, that they may join you and minister to you while you and your sons with you are before the tent of the testimony. They shall keep guard over you and over the whole tent, but shall not come near to the vessels of the sanctuary or to the altar lest they, and you, die. They shall join you and keep guard over the tent of meeting for all the service of the tent, and no outsider shall come near you. And you shall keep guard over the sanctuary and over the altar, that there may never again be wrath on the people of Israel. And behold, I have taken your brothers the Levites from among the people of Israel. They are a gift to you, given to the Lord, to do the service of the tent of meeting. And you and your sons with you shall guard your priesthood for all that concerns the altar and that is within the veil; and you shall serve. I give your priesthood as a gift, and any outsider who comes near shall be put to death" (Numbers 18:1–7).

Readers who joined this story with Korah's opening salvo in Numbers chapter 16 will infer that the Scripture passage above introduces a new dispensation for securing the tabernacle. Not so. This is a reiteration of the "Duties of the Levites" passage in Numbers 3:5–10, especially these details:

And the Lord spoke to Moses, saying, "Bring the tribe of Levi near, and set them before Aaron the priest ... . They shall keep guard over him and over the whole congregation before the tent of meeting ... . They shall ... keep guard over the people of Israel as they minister at the tabernacle. ... But if any outsider comes near, he shall be put to death.

This was a workable plan, but there are several reasons it stopped working. First, Eleazar, its point person was spread too thin. "And Eleazar the son of Aaron the priest was to be chief over the chiefs of the Levites, and to have oversight of those who kept guard over the sanctuary" (Numbers 3:32). His oversight of the tabernacle guards was not the first duty listed in his job description. He was squeezed between oversight's paradoxical definitions: the action of overseeing something; responsible and watchful care and an inadvertent omission or error; an unintentional failure to notice or do something.

Second, Eleazer's responsibilities included spiritual matters, which were fulfilling and prioritized but also temporal tasks, which could be mundane and menial. The latter tended to be put off when there was spiritual work that could be done instead. "And Eleazar ... shall have charge of the oil for the light, the fragrant incense, the regular grain offering, and the anointing oil, with the oversight of the whole tabernacle and all that is in it, of the sanctuary and its vessels" (Numbers 4:16).

Third, the priest population was now only 60 percent of what it was when the tabernacle opened. Subtract the high priest (who was in his mid-eighties at this point), and there were just half as many assistant priests as before. "So Eleazer and Ithamar served as priests in the lifetime of Aaron their father" (Numbers 3:4c). Eleazer had just one other priest in his job category.

Fourth, Eleazar's younger brother, Ithamar, evidently had fewer duties than Eleazar, which may have promoted sibling rivalry. His specific work is mentioned in only three other verses in the book of Numbers, then never again. By contrast, Numbers has many such references to Eleazar's duties. Ithamar may not have evidenced a strong work ethic. Anecdotally, older siblings in families throughout history have complained of heavy responsibilities their parents put on them, compared to the light loads lifted by their little brothers and sisters. All the birth order listings show Ithamar as Aaron's baby boy.

Finally, one of Ithamar's few job descriptions hints at where the original plan for tabernacle security may have faltered. Gershonites were one of the three divisions of Levites. "This is the service of the clans of the sons of the Gershonites in the tent of meeting, and their guard duty is to be under the direction of Ithamar the son of Aaron the priest" (Numbers 4:28).

Eleazar means "God is helper." God could see Eleazar was overworked and understaffed, so He helped him with the call for reinforcements (Numbers 18:1-7). This came the day after Korah's rebellion was put down, but his three sons survived. Biblical fact is clear that Korah's sons became the tabernacle doorkeepers. Much circumstantial evidence, plus absence of any hint of interim arrangements until they did, implies that they were the immediate and instant fulfillment. The Bible's earliest chronological naming of tabernacle gatekeepers names a descendant of Korah and traces this role back to his ancestors.

> Shallum the son of Kore, son of Ebiasaph, son of Korah, and his kinsmen … were in charge of the work of the service, keepers of the thresholds of the tent, as their fathers had been in charge of the camp of the LORD, keepers of the entrance. And Phineas the son of Eleazar was the chief officer over them in time past" (1 Chronicles 9:19–20).

The sons of Korah also testify of being the doorkeepers in the house of the Lord (Psalm 84:4, 10). Verse 10 links their tabernacle posts with the S.O.S. calls from God (Numbers 16:24) and Moses (16:26–27): "Depart from the tents of these wicked men, and touch nothing of theirs, lest you be swept away with all their sins."

In beefing up tabernacle security, God twice tells Aaron to bring his brothers from the tribe of Levi (Numbers 18:2, 6). Although all Levites were their tribal brothers, Korah's sons were now Aaron's next closest after Moses. Korah had been Aaron and Moses' first cousin, so his sons were their first cousins, once removed.

That Aaron's son Eleazar entered the Promised Land (Joshua 14:1; 24:33), as did Korah's sons, means all four were under twenty years old when Israel first refused to enter the Promised Land (Numbers 14:29). Cousins the same age who live in the same place know each other well and tend to be very close.

Aaron died in the wilderness at age 123 in the fifth month of Israel's final year there (Numbers 33:38–39). Eleazar ascended to high priest immediately. Numbers 34:17 says he would help Joshua divide the Promised Land to the tribes.

Throughout global history, regime changes at the top tend to bring personnel changes throughout the administration. God's foreknowledge that Eleazar would soon be high priest may have been a causative factor in his changing the tabernacle doorkeepers now. The Merarites had not performed well in this role, under Ithamar's management. The sons of Korah had shown their first and highest loyalty was to God-appointed people, principles, and procedures.

Although Assir, Abiasaph, and Elkanah did not meet the minimum age requirement for regular Levitical service, they would not be touching, handling, or carrying the sacred articles of the tent of meeting in their role as its doorkeepers. They had demonstrated their utmost respect for the things of the Lord and a spiritual maturity way beyond their years. Besides, they would serve under the watchful eyes of their uncles, Aaron and Moses.

The Phineas reference above has Phineas in charge of the tabernacle gatekeepers, which included Korah's son Abiasaph and his brothers. This would have begun in Numbers 33–34 when Phineas' father,

Eleazar, ascended as high priest at the death of his father, Aaron. This leaves little time between God's Numbers 18:4 call for gatekeepers and Phineas supervising the sons of Korah in this role. This, plus the fact that Scripture never mentions any other gatekeepers after Korah's rebellion, leads to the reasonable conclusion that the sons of Korah stepped into this role a day or so after their father's death. And they grew to love it.

> *For a day in your courts is better than a thousand elsewhere. I would rather be a doorkeeper in the house of my God than dwell in the tents of wickedness (Psalm 84:10).*

PART TWO

VICTORS: THE SONGS OF THE SONS OF KORAH

PSALM 88

A SONG. A PSALM OF THE SONS OF KORAH.
A MASKIL OF HEMAN THE EZRAHITE.

¹O LORD, God of my salvation,
I cry out day and night before you.
²Let my prayer come before you;
incline your ear to my cry!

³For my soul is full of troubles,
and my life draws near to Sheol.
⁴I am counted among those who go down to the pit;
I am a man who has no strength,
⁵like one set loose among the dead,
like the slain that lie in the grave,
like those whom you remember no more,
for they are cut off from your hand.
⁶You have put me in the depths of the pit,
in the regions dark and deep.
⁷Your wrath lies heavy upon me,
and you overwhelm me with all your waves. — Selah

⁸You have caused my companions to shun me;
you have made me a horror to them.
I am shut in so that I cannot escape;
⁹my eye grows dim through sorrow.

Every day I call upon you, O LORD;
I spread out my hands to you.
¹⁰*Do you work wonders for the dead?*
Do the departed rise up to praise you? — Selah

¹¹*Is your steadfast love declared in the grave,*
or your faithfulness in Abaddon?
¹²*Are your wonders known in the darkness,*
or your righteousness in the land of forgetfulness?

¹³*But I, O LORD, cry to you;*
in the morning my prayer comes before you.
¹⁴*O LORD, why do you cast my soul away?*
Why do you hide your face from me?
¹⁵*Afflicted and close to death from my youth up,*
I suffer your terrors; I am helpless.
¹⁶*Your wrath has swept over me;*
your dreadful assaults destroy me.
¹⁷*They surround me like a flood all day long;*
they close in on me together.
¹⁸*You have caused my beloved and my friend to shun me;*
my companions have become darkness.

This psalm's tone and anguish, and especially its content, make this most likely the first psalm composed by the sons of Korah. Most of their other psalms have added references to later periods in Israel's history, but everything in Psalm 88 reflects the wilderness period before the Canaan entry. It uses first person singular thirty-four times but never first-person plural. This implies that one of the trio composed the words.

Because it struck a nerve with his brothers, the writer would have learned it from the tune in which he sang or chanted it. Being sung helped this psalm be passed down orally through the generations. Later sons of Korah would not have sung it with the same pathos and pain but as a lament to the ordeal that launched its charter members as their initiation fee.

Modern readers may take offense at its complaints against God. This is common throughout the book of Psalms, many of which have verses written in first and second person, as is this whole psalm.

God does not take offense. Our personal relationship with Him is based on honesty, which allows it to grow. Korah's sons vented the horror and deep grief they experienced over how their parents were taken from them. God was able to heal their hurts and move them to be able to forgive, trust, love and praise Him. Are there hurts in your life that you have never poured out honestly to your heavenly Father? This psalm gives you the example and encouragement to do so, since all Scripture is inspired by God (2 Timothy 3:16).

The Bible attributes this psalm's final form to Heman. He became the second most famous of the sons of Korah after his grandfather Samuel (judge, prophet, priest). Heman means "faithful." He probably added "Selah" at the end of verses 7 and 10. This is a musical notation, similar to a rest, and calls the hearer or reader to ponder the clause it follows.

Heman was the first of the three chief Levites to whom was entrusted the conduct of the vocal and instrumental music of the tabernacle in David's time and later in the temple (1 Chronicles 6:31–48). David knew how Levites proudly traced their history back to Levi's three sons, so he appointed Heman from the Kohathites, Asaph from the Gershomites, and Ethan from the Merarites. David appointed these musicians when he brought back the tent of meeting from its Philistine captivity. Their grandest performance was to lead the music and praise when Solomon completed and dedicated the temple.

Asaph was the more prolific songwriter (twelve psalms to Heman's one), but Heman was the greater musician. He, not Asaph, was called "singer" (i.e. musician) in 1 Chronicles 6:33. Heman's fourteen sons are named in 1 Chronicles 25:4, followed by the Bible's best tribute to him:

> *All these were the sons of Heman the king's seer, according to the promise of God to exalt him, for God had given Heman fourteen sons and three daughters. They were all under the direction of their father in the music in the house of the LORD with cymbals, harps, and lyres for the service of the house of God (1 Chronicles 25:5–6b).*

Psalm 88:6 ends with the Hebrew word *Abbadon*, one name for the abode of the dead, which some Bible versions translate as "Destruction." *Sheol* in verse 3 is the Hebrew name for where the souls of all the departed dead go. This is the third of sixty-six Old Testament uses (after Jacob in Genesis 27:35 and 44:29). These three typify the Old Testament's nebulous and undeveloped theology of the afterlife.

Korah's sons' grief was magnified by their parents' sudden death, which bypassed the endearing presence of a family tomb. *Sheol* is translated "hell" thirty-one times in the Old Testament, the first in Deuteronomy 32:22 — Moses' last sermon (called "song" in 31:30) to his people. *Sheol*/Hell, in context here, seems to describe the consuming fire of God's wrath on the earth:

> *They have made me jealous with what is no god; they have provoked me to anger with their idols. So I will make them jealous with those who are no people; I will provoke them to anger with*

a foolish nation. For a fire is kindled by my anger, and it burns to
the depths of Sheol, devours the earth and its increase, and sets on
fire the foundations of the mountains (Deuteronomy 32:21–22).

The Old Testament renders *Sheol* informally as "the pit." (4, 6). What happened to Korah, Dathan, and Abiram is the epitome illustration of this. The New Testament clarifies and details the afterlife in Luke 16:19–31.

Jesus calls it *Hades*, the Greek translation of *Sheol*. His most important revelations here are: 1) It is divided into two compartments, which eternally separate the righteous and the wicked dead. 2) The wicked dead can see the righteous dead but cannot go to them. 3) The wicked are in a place of torment, anguish, and flame. 4) Those in this torment want their living relatives to be warned, so they do not share this fate.

I exhort you to read Luke 16:19–31 seriously. If this leaves any question about your eternal destination, turn to "The Romans Road" in this book's appendices. If you have acquaintances whom you suspect are headed for the place of torment, encourage them to read Luke 16:19-31. If they want to do something about it, share "The Romans Road" with them.

Psalm 84

A Psalm of the Sons of Korah

^{1}How lovely is your dwelling place,
O Lord of hosts!
^{2}My soul longs, yes, faints
for the courts of the Lord;
my heart and flesh sing for joy
to the living God.

^{3}Even the sparrow finds a home,
and the swallow a nest for herself,
where she may lay her young,
at your altars, O Lord of hosts,
my king and my God.
^{4}Blessed are those who dwell in your house,
ever singing your praise! — Selah

^{5}Blessed are those whose strength is in you,
in whose heart are the highways to Zion.
^{6}As they go through the Valley of Baca
they make it a place of springs;
the early rain also covers it with pools.
^{7}They go from strength to strength;
each one appears before God in Zion.

⁸O LORD God of hosts, hear my prayer;
give ear, O God of Jacob! — Selah
⁹Behold our shield, O God;
look on the face of your anointed!

¹⁰For a day in your courts is better
than a thousand elsewhere.
I would rather be a doorkeeper in the house of my God
than dwell in the tents of wickedness.
¹¹For the LORD God is a sun and shield;
the LORD bestows favor and honor.
No good thing does he withhold
from those who walk uprightly.
¹²O LORD of hosts,
blessed is the one who trusts in you!

This psalm of the sons of Korah pairs easily with Psalm 88. It too has a primary lyricist, using "my" six times and "I" once but "our" or "we" only in verse 9. These two psalms bookend the two coming-of-age events for Korah's sons: losing their parents but gaining their posts as tabernacle gatekeepers. Verse 10b contrasts these, valuing a small position in God's house, once their father led the rebellion against God's authority. The last words they heard before their family tent disappeared with their parents in it was: "Depart from the tents of these wicked men" (Numbers 16:26, NLT). They esteemed the quality of one day of lowly service in God's anointing over the quantity of one thousand days in the best the world could offer.

They loved being near God. "How lovely is your dwelling place" (1). "My soul longs for the courts of the LORD; heart and flesh sing for joy to the living God" (2). "Blessed are those who dwell in your house, ever singing your praise!" (4).

Do you love spending time alone with God each day? Do you look forward to Sundays when you can worship with the Lord's people and sing His praises? Is there any place you had rather be than at church?

Life is a challenge. "Blessed are those whose strength is in you" (5a). Life is a journey, but peaceful travel for those in whose heart are the highways to Zion (5b). Life's highways have some depressions, but we can minister to others there as our Father lovingly pats the tears on our cheeks.

"As they go through the Valley of Baca, they make it a place of springs" (6a). There is no valley in Israel or the wilderness by this name, which means weeping or tears, but the lowest times in our life show it on our faces. Others face them too, so we can help make it a place of springs for them. As we move through the pain, we can look for the gain. "No good thing does he withhold from those who walk uprightly" (11).

"Selah" has been added at the ends of verses 4 and 8, neatly breaking this dozen-verse song into three stanzas. A writer from King David's time or later also added "Zion," a name for Jerusalem on Mount Zion, at the end of verse 7. This is where they went for the three annual feasts of the Lord. Those living close enough also went there on weekly Sabbaths.

PSALM 46

OF THE SONS OF KORAH

¹*God is our refuge and strength,*
a very present help in trouble.
²*Therefore we will not fear though the earth gives way,*
though the mountains be moved into the heart of the sea,
³*though its waters roar and foam,*
though the mountains tremble at its swelling. — *Selah*

⁴*There is a river whose streams make glad the city of God,*
the holy habitation of the Most High.
⁵*God is in the midst of her; she shall not be moved;*
God will help her when morning dawns.
⁶*The nations rage, the kingdoms totter;*
he utters his voice, the earth melts.
⁷*The* LORD *of hosts is with us;*
the God of Jacob is our fortress. — *Selah*

⁸*Come, behold the works of the* LORD,
how he has brought desolations on the earth.
⁹*He makes wars cease to the end of the earth;*
he breaks the bow and shatters the spear;
he burns the chariots with fire.
¹⁰*"Be still, and know that I am God.*
I will be exalted among the nations,

I will be exalted in the earth!"
[11] *The LORD of hosts is with us;*
  the God of Jacob is our fortress. — Selah

This psalm's first two verses are exclusively the literal testimony of Korah's sons. "The earth melts" (6) and "desolations on the earth" could allude to the earth giving way. They have progressed from angry outrage over how their parents died to grateful testimony that God succeeded their human parents as their help, strength, and refuge. They have harmonized on this song, which uses the first person six times in the plural but never in the singular. They are now a "we" with their earthly brothers and heavenly Father.

Like much music, there are repeats in this song. "Selah" ends verses 3, 7, and 11, noting the song's three stanzas. The last two end with "the LORD of hosts is with us; the God of Jacob is our fortress." "The city of God" is not called Zion or Jerusalem, dating this to an earlier period. For this trio, the tent of meeting was "the holy habitation of the Most High." Their life was a story of fear to faith.

Using this song and a few other verses, here's how your life can be, too.

Stepping from Fear to Faith

- God's **protection**. God's *refuge* is the place we go when the bottom falls out on us (1, 7, 11).
- God's **presence**. God's refuge (*very present help*, 1) is the person we know when the bottom falls out. God is *in the midst* of her (5). The Lord of Hosts is with us (7, 11).
- God's **peace of mind** (*will not fear*, 2; *be still and know*, 10). Read Philippians 4:4–7.
- God's **pleasure** (*make glad*, 4).

- God's **permanence** (*shall not be moved*, 5).
- God's **punctuality** (*early*, 5).
- God's **proof** (*behold the works of the Lord*, 8).
- God's **peacemaking** (*makes wars to cease*, 9).
-

Staying from Fear to Faith

Repetition: Verse 7 repeats as verse 11. What in your life needs more practice?

Relationship: "The God of Jacob is our refuge (7, 11).

Richness: Psalm 46 uses two different nouns for refuge: *machseh* (1) and *misgab* (7, 11). The Old Testament uses three more: *manos* (2 Samuel 22:3; Psalms 59:16; 142:4; Jeremiah 16:19), *meonah* (Deuteronomy 33:27), and *miglat* (Numbers 35 has ten references to "cities of refuge," which the Lord is for us).

Different people need different refuge, and individuals need different refuge at different times. Psalm 57:1 uses a different word, *chasah*: "Be merciful to me, O God, be merciful to me, for in you my soul takes refuge; in the shadow of your wings I will take refuge, till the storms of destruction pass by."

Relish: *Selah*. Ponder, meditate on, take advantage of, and be thankful for ways that God is your refuge.

"Therefore, we will not fear, though … ." Faith is the seesaw between your "though" and your "therefore."

Psalm 42

Of the Sons of Korah

¹*As a deer pants for flowing streams,*
so pants my soul for you, O God.
²*My soul thirsts for God,*
for the living God.
When shall I come and appear before God?
³*My tears have been my food*
day and night,
while they say to me all the day long,
"Where is your God?"
⁴*These things I remember,*
as I pour out my soul:
how I would go with the throng
and lead them in procession to the house of God
with glad shouts and songs of praise,
a multitude keeping festival.

⁵*Why are you cast down, O my soul,*
and why are you in turmoil within me?
Hope in God; for I shall again praise him,
my salvation and my God.

⁶*My soul is cast down within me;*
therefore I remember you

from the land of Jordan and of Hermon,
from Mount Mizar.
⁷Deep calls to deep
at the roar of your waterfalls;
all your breakers and your waves
have gone over me.
⁸By day the LORD commands his steadfast love,
and at night his song is with me,
a prayer to the God of my life.
⁹I say to God, my rock:
"Why have you forgotten me?
Why do I go mourning
because of the oppression of the enemy?"
¹⁰As with a deadly wound in my bones,
my adversaries taunt me,
while they say to me all the day long,
"Where is your God?"

¹¹Why are you cast down, O my soul,
and why are you in turmoil within me?
Hope in God; for I shall again praise him,
my salvation and my God.

This song pairs nicely with Psalm 84, which uses the first person seven times in the singular with a lone plural use. Psalm 42 avoids first person plural but uses its singular thirty-two times in just eleven verses. It echoes and expands the 84:5 reference to "the highways to Zion" with "I would go with the throng and lead them in procession to the house of God with glad shouts and songs of praise, a multitude keeping festival" (4b).

Being forever called sons of Korah brought some baggage, the notoriety of their namesake. It brought taunts: "My tears have been my food day and night, while they say to me all day long, 'Where is your God?'" (3).

This was a recurring nightmare: "'Why have you forgotten me? Why do I go mourning because of the oppression of the enemy?' As with a deadly wound in my bones, my adversaries taunt me, while they say to me all the day long, 'Where is your God?'" (9b–10).

It dredges up how Korah's sons first blamed God: "All your breakers and waves have gone over me" (7b). They had to periodically reassure themselves and reaffirm their faith in and love for God.

So a fifth of this psalm is their question and answer repeated in the middle and the end of the song: "Why are you cast down, O my soul, and why are you in turmoil within me? Hope in God; for I shall again praise him, my salvation and my God" (5, 11).

To overcome the doubts, they had to recall this, day and night: "By day the LORD commands his steadfast love, and at night his song is with me, a prayer to the God of my life" (8).

The end effect of this recalibration was peace of mind, which brings the thirst for God and hunger for His presence with which they begin this psalm: "As a deer pants for flowing streams, so pants my soul for you, O God. My soul thirsts for God, for the living God. When shall I come and appear before God" (1–2)?

As New Covenant believers indwelt by the Holy Spirit, having our personal copies of God's word in several versions, we can appear before God almost at will. He waits for us. "Let us then with confidence draw near to the throne of grace, that we may receive mercy and find grace to help in time of need" (Hebrews 4:16).

PSALM 43

TO THE CHOIRMASTER. A MASKIL OF THE SONS OF KORAH.

¹*Vindicate me, O God, and defend my cause*
against an ungodly people,
from the deceitful and unjust man
deliver me!
²*For you are the God in whom I take refuge;*
why have you rejected me?
Why do I go about mourning
because of the oppression of the enemy?

³*Send out your light and your truth;*
let them lead me;
let them bring me to your holy hill
and to your dwelling!
⁴*Then I will go to the altar of God,*
to God my exceeding joy,
and I will praise you with the lyre,
O God, my God.

⁵*Why are you cast down, O my soul,*
and why are you in turmoil within me?
Hope in God; for I shall again praise him,
my salvation and my God.

Unless you use the NIV Life Application Bible, yours probably does not credit Psalm 43 to the sons of Korah. Hebrew Bibles do, but as the third stanza of Psalm 42. The chorus ending this stanza is verses 5 and 11 in Psalm 42. These Siamese twin psalms were split in the mid-third century BC in Egypt when its king wanted a Greek Old Testament for his library.

Even Jews in Israel needed the Bible in Greek, since most could speak Aramaic and Greek but not Hebrew. Greek Old Testaments are called *Septuagint*, meaning seventy, since it took about that many scholars to get a good translation. It was not **the** *Septuagint* but the collections of many Greek translations being done. **Many** Old Testament quotes in the New are actually from Greek, not Hebrew, since the Old Testament scriptures of the early church were *Septuagint*.

The Hebrew word *maskil* literally means "enlightened." Such songs were composed to communicate, not just celebrate. Like Psalm 42, this psalm is first person singular (seventeen times in five verses) with first person plural not used. The psalmist is venting his own anger at God (2) because people are mistreating him (1–2). Today, we tend to be that way, too, This short psalm hinges on its middle verse 3.

If God will enlighten, lead, and welcome him, then he will worship, praise, and rejoice in God (4). He talks to himself in the chorus in the midst of despair and disturbance. He reminds himself that God is his hope, so he should resume his praise and reaffirm his salvation. When we are battling back after the bottom has fallen out on us, these are the types of talks we need to have with ourselves. The original sons of Korah heard Uncle Moses preach, "You shall love the LORD your God with all your heart and with all your soul and with all your might" (Deuteronomy 6:5). His next sermon they heard asked, "What does the LORD require of you, but to fear the LORD your God, to walk in all his ways, to love him, to serve the LORD your God with all your heart and with all your soul" (10:12).

Moses' first sermon stressed to pass these priorities to your children: "And these words that I command you today shall be on your heart. You shall teach them diligently to your children" (6:6–7). The sons of Korah did such a good job passing this down that centuries later the writer of Psalms 42 and 43 had a guilty conscience when his soul was not in tune with God. It stressed him out until he got right with the Lord again.

Centuries later, Jesus was asked which is the greatest commandment in the law. The Son of God was not a son of Korah, but He answered, "You shall love the Lord your God with all your heart and with all your soul and with all your mind. This is the great and first commandment" (Matthew 22:36–38).

Soul is our personality and is composed of our mind, will, and emotions. In the life of this son of Korah as with us, emotions often grow way out of proportion, especially in tough times. Romans 12:2 exhorts us to not be conformed to the world ("don't be like everyone else") but be transformed by the renewing of our mind. The best way to renew our mind is to fill it with God's Word. Memorize it and meditate on it.

PSALM 44

A MASKIL OF THE SONS OF KORAH

¹O God, we have heard with our ears,

our fathers have told us,

what deeds you performed in their days,

in the days of old:

²you with your own hand drove out the nations,

but them you planted;

you afflicted the peoples,

but them you set free;

³for not by their own sword did they win the land,

nor did their own arm save them,

but your right hand and your arm,

and the light of your face,

for you delighted in them.

⁴You are my King, O God;

ordain salvation for Jacob!

⁵Through you we push down our foes;

through your name we tread down those who rise up against us.

⁶For not in my bow do I trust,

nor can my sword save me.

⁷But you have saved us from our foes

and have put to shame those who hate us.

⁸In God we have boasted continually,

and we will give thanks to your name forever. — Selah

. . . .

⁹But you have rejected us and disgraced us
and have not gone out with our armies.
¹⁰You have made us turn back from the foe,
and those who hate us have gotten spoil.
¹¹You have made us like sheep for slaughter
and have scattered us among the nations.
¹²You have sold your people for a trifle,
demanding no high price for them.
¹³You have made us the taunt of our neighbors,
the derision and scorn of those around us.
¹⁴You have made us a byword among the nations,
a laughingstock among the peoples.
¹⁵All day long my disgrace is before me,
and shame has covered my face
¹⁶at the sound of the taunter and reviler,
at the sight of the enemy and the avenger.

. . . .

¹⁷All this has come upon us,
though we have not forgotten you,
and we have not been false to your covenant.
¹⁸Our heart has not turned back,
nor have our steps departed from your way;

. . . .

¹⁹yet you have broken us in the place of jackals
and covered us with the shadow of death.
²⁰If we had forgotten the name of our God
or spread out our hands to a foreign god,
²¹would not God discover this?
For he knows the secrets of the heart.

²²Yet for your sake we are killed all the day long;
we are regarded as sheep to be slaughtered.
²³Awake! Why are you sleeping, O LORD?
Rouse yourself! Do not reject us forever!
²⁴Why do you hide your face?
Why do you forget our affliction and oppression?
²⁵For our soul is bowed down to the dust;
our belly clings to the ground.

. . . .

So: *²⁶Rise up; come to our help!*
Redeem us for the sake of your steadfast love!

Psalm 44 is a communal lament. Its spokesman uses the first-person plural thirty-five times. Glance up at the first two words in verses 9–14 for a machine-gun burst of charges against God. My dotted lines above break the psalm into its five movements. In good times, you can stop with the thanks.

When the bottom has fallen out on you, you can identify with and use the rest of this song. Don't be afraid or ashamed to admit something to God. Verse 21 reveals that He already knows your secrets. Verse 22 may sound familiar and is quoted in Romans 8:36. The best passage for battling back may be Romans 8:16–39. (For a great sermon on Psalm 44, visit living-faith.org/2017/10/18/psalm-44-when-god-is-silent.)

Psalms 44:24 and 88:14 are the sons' two mentions of God hiding His face — a great study when the bottom falls out. For further references, see Deuteronomy 31:17–18; 32:20; Job 34:29; Psalm 10:11; 13:1; 22:24; 27:9; 30:7; 44:24; 51:9; 69:17; 102:2;104:29; 143:7; Isaiah 8:17; 54:8; 59:2; 64:7; Jeremiah 33:5; Ezekiel 39:23–24; and Micah 3:4. In Ezekiel 39:29, God promises, "I will not hide my face anymore from them when I pour out my Spirit." *Selah!*

PSALM 85

A PSALM OF THE SONS OF KORAH

¹LORD, you were favorable to your land;

you restored the fortunes of Jacob.

²You forgave the iniquity of your people;

you covered all their sin. — Selah

³You withdrew all your wrath;

you turned from your hot anger.

⁴Restore us again, O God of our salvation,

and put away your indignation toward us!

⁵Will you be angry with us forever?

Will you prolong your anger to all generations?

⁶Will you not revive us again,

that your people may rejoice in you?

⁷Show us your steadfast love, O LORD,

and grant us your salvation.

⁸Let me hear what God the LORD will speak,

for he will speak peace to his people, to his saints;

but let them not turn back to folly.

⁹Surely his salvation is near to those who fear him,

that glory may dwell in our land.

¹⁰Steadfast love and faithfulness meet;

righteousness and peace kiss each other.
[11]Faithfulness springs up from the ground,
and righteousness looks down from the sky.
[12]Yes, the LORD will give what is good,
and our land will yield its increase.
[13]Righteousness will go before him
and make his footsteps a way.

This writer speaks only to God in the first half of the psalm. He speaks for his people in verses 4–7. He speaks for himself in the first third of verse 8, then to his people about God the last half of the song. I have broken the above text to show these parts, which may have been written at different times. In part one, the land is God's; in part three, the land is theirs. No reference to the wilderness or conquering the land east or west of the Jordan River dates this psalm to the monarchy (the reigns of Saul, David, Solomon).

Verse 11 pictures their faithfulness from the ground in response to God's righteousness from the sky. The verb form of "revive" in verse 6 mirrors this. "Revive" is rare in the Old Testament, used just ten times and only the word *chayah*. Verse 6 above is its passive form, "to be revived," which outside of its two appearances in Psalms is used only after their seventy-year exile in Babylon. The verb's middle voice is used only after the exile, and Isaiah 57:15 is the lone use of active voice. Only God can revive, which the Korah psalmist knows they need, because of their iniquity, sin (2), and folly (8).

Steadfast love (7, 9) is a special concept in the Old Testament. It is unique to God, like *agape* love in the New Testament. Sometimes translated "loving kindness," it is one Hebrew word, *chesed*. But no one word in English can say it all. In verses 9–13, God's attributes (*chesed*, faithfulness, righteousness, peace) take on a life of their own and become the subjects of active verbs. Many Bible scholars, theologians, and preachers have seen Jesus as the perfect fulfillment of verse 10 in His earthly life and death.

God's wrath and hot anger (3) and indignation (4) were shown in Korah's story. His sons show that God does not prolong His anger to all generations (5). When you are battling back from the bottom falling out on you, as they did, start with verse 8, "Let me hear what God the LORD will speak." He "will speak peace to you" because you are His. "His salvation is near you" because you fear Him with reverential awe (9). When you were saved, you experienced through Christ His salvation from the penalty of your sin.

As you battle back from the bottom falling out, God's steadfast love can heal you from the hurts our fallen world has inflicted on you. The Lord will give you what is good. When we love God and are committed to His purpose, He works all things together for our good. *Selah.*

PSALM 45

To the Choirmaster: According to the Lilies.
A Maschil of the Sons of Korah; A Love Song.

¹My heart overflows with a pleasing theme;
I address my verses to the king;
my tongue is like the pen of a ready scribe.

²You are the most handsome of the sons of men;
grace is poured upon your lips;
therefore God has blessed you forever.
³Gird your sword on your thigh, O mighty one,
in your splendor and majesty!

⁴In your majesty ride out victoriously
for the cause of truth and meekness and righteousness;
let your right hand teach you awesome deeds!
⁵Your arrows are sharp
in the heart of the king's enemies;
the peoples fall under you.

⁶Your throne, O God, is forever and ever.
The scepter of your kingdom is a scepter of uprightness;
⁷you have loved righteousness and hated wickedness.
Therefore God, your God, has anointed you
with the oil of gladness beyond your companions;

8your robes are all fragrant with myrrh and aloes and cassia.
From ivory palaces stringed instruments make you glad;
9daughters of kings are among your ladies of honor;
at your right hand stands the queen in gold of Ophir.

10Hear, O daughter, and consider, and incline your ear:
forget your people and your father's house,
11and the king will desire your beauty.
Since he is your lord, bow to him.
12The people of Tyre will seek your favor with gifts,
the richest of the people.

13All glorious is the princess in her chamber, with robes interwoven
    with gold.
14In many-colored robes she is led to the king,
with her virgin companions following behind her.
15With joy and gladness they are led along
as they enter the palace of the king.

16In place of your fathers shall be your sons;
you will make them princes in all the earth.
17I will cause your name to be remembered in all generations;
therefore nations will praise you forever and ever.

The last five psalms the sons of Korah wrote seem to fit the reigns of David and Solomon. These were the heydays for the sons of Korah when their office became more visible, valuable, and musical. The bookend events were David's return of the tent of meeting — turning it into a place of worship — and Solomon's dedication of the temple in the population center of Jerusalem. Its dedication was the Levites' grandest hour.

Parts of this psalm are clear references to David, Israel's warrior king (3–5). Verse 6 hints of God's promise to perpetuate David's reign through his descendants. Verse 7b recalls David's anointing over his seven older brothers. Verse 7a contrasts David's honorable reign after Saul's miserable one. Verse 8 seems to begin a later composition rehearsing the peaceful, luxurious reign of Solomon.

Today's Christians have not mined the gold in this psalm. Dr. Jerry Vines says, "Psalm 45 provides a beautiful pre-picture of the future marriage supper of the Lamb" (email to author, 4/26/23). Meditate on it from this perspective.

Americans spent hours watching the 2023 coronation of Great Britain's new king. Use this imagery to picture God as your King. Meditate on Psalm 45's many allusions to our King of kings. Sing or read the great hymn, "Crown Him with Many Crowns."

Jesus teaches us to pray, "Your kingdom come, your will be done, on earth as it is in heaven" (Matthew 6:10). Christ Himself is the King of kings and Lord of lords (1 Timothy 6:15; Revelation 17:14; 19:16). In the synoptic gospels, Jesus speaks of His kingdom fifty times in Matthew, sixteen times in Mark, and thirty-six times in Luke.

The Sons of Korah begin this psalm with, "My heart overflows with a pleasing theme; I address my verses to the king." When the bottom has fallen out on us, our heart is on empty. As we address our thoughts and words to our King, He can begin to shift our focus from our problems to His peace and plans.

PSALM 47

TO THE CHOIRMASTER. A PSALM OF THE SONS OF KORAH.

¹Clap your hands, all peoples!
Shout to God with loud songs of joy!
²For the LORD, the Most High, is to be feared,
a great king over all the earth.
³He subdued peoples under us,
and nations under our feet.
⁴He chose our heritage for us,
the pride of Jacob whom he loves. — Selah

⁵God has gone up with a shout,
the LORD with the sound of a trumpet.
⁶Sing praises to God, sing praises!
Sing praises to our king, sing praises!
⁷For God is the king of all the earth;
sing praises with a psalm!

⁸God reigns over the nations;
God sits on his holy throne.
⁹The princes of the peoples gather
as the people of the God of Abraham.
For the shields of the earth belong to God;
he is highly exalted!

Psalm 47:2, 6, and 7 expand Psalm 45's focus on God as King. Psalm 47 mentions His throne (8) and extends His reign over all the earth (2) and the nations (8). It calls all peoples to fear Him (2) and to worship Him expressively with joy (1). Verse 6 is a quartet of commands to sing praises to our King.

Within this global worship, Israel remains His special people, the psalm naming two of their three patriarchs. Jacob (renamed Israel, "ruling with God") is God's pride and love. Earth's princes gather as the people of the God of Abraham, fulfilling God's plan and prophecy in Genesis 12:3: "In you all the families of the earth shall be blessed." The pleasant paradox of evangelism and missions is that multiplying God's global children never diminishes your relationship with Him.

Liturgical and traditional churches who stress the respectful reverence of worship are called and commanded to balance this reverence with clapping, shouts, and loud songs of joy. Our God is both transcendent (seen in God the Father) and imminent (displayed by the incarnate and risen Son). A transcendent God is worshiped by reverence, and an imminent God is worshiped by celebration, so our Trinitarian worship calls for a blend of both.

Unlike some of the Songs of the sons of Korah, Psalm 47 is totally positive and upbeat, making no charges or complaints against God. Worship means ascribing worth to God, so this is worship at its highest and best. When the bottom falls out on us, it is tough for us to praise God totally with no mention of our disappointments. Genuineness and honesty in our relationship with God require that we start with catharsis, getting things off our chest, as the sons of Korah did in Psalm 88, the first song they wrote.

But battling back bids us to at least praise God for something. We can always praise Him for our salvation long ago and our heavenly future with Him. As we progress in battling back, our praise meter should rise, and our rants should reduce. If we cannot honestly thank God **for** all things (Ephesians 5:20), we can at least thank Him **in** everything (1 Thessalonians 5:18). "And we know that for those who love God all things work together for good, for those who are called according to his purpose" (Romans 8: 28).

In 1997 Chris Machen wrote "Bow the Knee," tune by Mike Harland. It's my favorite song to sing in our church choir, because it touches the pain and pathos of the believer's life on earth. Here's part of it:

> "There are moments in our journey following the Lord where God illumines ev'ry step we take. There are times when circumstances make perfect sense to us, As we try to understand each move He makes. When the path grows dim and our questions have no answers, turn to Him. Bow the knee: Trust the heart of your Father when the answer goes beyond what you can see. Bow the knee; Lift your eyes toward heaven and believe the One who holds eternity. And when you don't understand the purpose of His plan, in the presence of the King, bow the knee." (CCLI License #207101).

PSALM 48

A SONG. A PSALM OF THE SONS OF KORAH.

¹*Great is the LORD and greatly to be praised*
in the city of our God!
His holy mountain,
²*beautiful in elevation,*
is the joy of all the earth,
Mount Zion, in the far north,
the city of the great King.
³*Within her citadels God*
has made himself known as a fortress.

⁴*For behold, the kings assembled;*
they came on together.
⁵*As soon as they saw it, they were astounded;*
they were in panic; they took to flight.
⁶*Trembling took hold of them there,*
anguish as of a woman in labor.
⁷*By the east wind you shattered*
the ships of Tarshish.
⁸*As we have heard, so have we seen*
in the city of the LORD of hosts,
in the city of our God,
which God will establish forever. — Selah

⁹*We have thought on your steadfast love, O God,*
in the midst of your temple.
¹⁰*As your name, O God,*
so your praise reaches to the ends of the earth.
Your right hand is filled with righteousness.
¹¹*Let Mount Zion be glad!*
Let the daughters of Judah rejoice
because of your judgments!

¹²*Walk about Zion, go around her,*
number her towers,
¹³*consider well her ramparts,*
go through her citadels,
that you may tell the next generation
¹⁴*that this is God,*
our God forever and ever.
He will guide us forever.

A Gentile believer's version of this psalm would be verses 10 and 14 plus eighteen words: the first nine in verses 1 and 9. The other twelve verses plus the last nine words in verse 1 and the last six words in verse 9 are about Mount Zion.

So what's the big deal about Jerusalem? I googled this question to see how close my wording would come to a real article. It was written October 17, 2018, by an Aussie as his country considered following the lead of the U.S. in moving its embassy to Jerusalem from Tel Aviv. I do not recommend this article, so here are my answers from a half century of serious Bible study.

- God loves Jerusalem, so we should. He put this word in the Bible over 800 times (over 140 in the New Testament), plus all the times

He referred to it by other names, such as Zion or Mount Zion on 150 occasions.

- Jesus died for the sins of the world in Jerusalem, just outside where the city wall was then.

- Jesus rose from the dead there, which declared Him to be the Son of God in power (Romans 1:4).

- It was in Jerusalem that Jesus instituted the Lord's Supper, which proclaims His death until He comes (1 Corinthians 11:26).

- Jerusalem is where God first sent the Holy Spirit to indwell believers and empower their witness (Acts 1–2).

- Jerusalem is where Jesus will return to earth on the Mount of Olives, just east of the city wall (Zechariah 14:4).

- Jerusalem is where Abraham took Isaac, his beloved son, to sacrifice him. This event pictures the cross (Genesis 22).

- Jerusalem is where David, who served God's purpose in his generation (Acts 13:36), put Israel's capital.

- The Great Commission's fulfillment started in Jerusalem (Luke 24:47; Acts 1:8).

- God's inspired Word in verse 8 calls it "the city of the LORD of hosts, the city of our God, which God will establish forever."

- Deacons were first chosen in Jerusalem to take the administrative load off the apostles (Acts 6).

- It was in Jerusalem where Jewish believers decided that Gentiles could become Christians without first becoming Jews (Acts 15).

- Jerusalem is where the first Christian martyr gave his life (Stephen, Acts 7:54–60).

- It was from Jerusalem that the risen Christ ascended back into heaven (Acts 1:6–12).

- It was in Jerusalem where Christian prayer meetings began (Acts 1:12–14, 2:42, 4:23–31, 12:5–12).

PSALM 49

To the Choirmaster. A Psalm of the Sons of Korah.

¹Hear this, all peoples!
Give ear, all inhabitants of the world,
²both low and high,
rich and poor together!
³My mouth shall speak wisdom;
the meditation of my heart shall be understanding.
⁴I will incline my ear to a proverb;
I will solve my riddle to the music of the lyre.

⁵Why should I fear in times of trouble,
when the iniquity of those who cheat me surrounds me,
⁶those who trust in their wealth
and boast of the abundance of their riches?
⁷Truly no man can ransom another,
or give to God the price of his life,
⁸for the ransom of their life is costly
and can never suffice,
⁹that he should live on forever
and never see the pit.

¹⁰For he sees that even the wise die;
the fool and the stupid alike must perish
and leave their wealth to others.

¹¹*Their graves are their homes forever,*
their dwelling places to all generations,
though they called lands by their own names.
¹²*Man in his pomp will not remain;*
he is like the beasts that perish.

¹³*This is the path of those who have foolish confidence;*
yet after them people approve of their boasts. — Selah

¹⁴*Like sheep they are appointed for Sheol;*
death shall be their shepherd,
and the upright shall rule over them in the morning.
Their form shall be consumed in Sheol, with no place to dwell.
¹⁵*But God will ransom my soul from the power of Sheol,*
for he will receive me. — Selah

¹⁶*Be not afraid when a man becomes rich,*
when the glory of his house increases.
¹⁷*For when he dies he will carry nothing away;*
his glory will not go down after him.
¹⁸*For though, while he lives, he counts himself blessed —*
and though you get praise when you do well for yourself —
¹⁹*his soul will go to the generation of his fathers,*
who will never again see light.
²⁰*Man in his pomp yet without understanding is like the beasts*
that perish.

Verse 4 is the lone mention of a proverb in the psalms of the sons of Korah, which pegs it to the life and literature of Solomon. The pinnacles in Jewish history date to Solomon and his father David, Israel's two most famous kings. The musical role of the sons of Korah was multiplied by the praise procession when David brought back the Tent of Meeting. Their grandest showcase was launched by the dedication of the temple built by Solomon.

This psalm has a somber tone, almost morbid. It harks to the event which brought notoriety to the sons of Korah, the judgmental death of their rebellious father. This psalm bookends Psalm 88, when their grief over this event was still fresh and raw. It is more philosophical here.

Both psalms mention the Old Testament's two main names for the place of the departed dead: *Sheol* (14, 15) and "the pit" (9). It has a dozen references to life and death, plus two to God's control over both.

This psalm addresses the whole world, as all its inhabitants face death. It warns those who trust in earthly fame, fortune, or intellect (6–8, 10–13, 16–18). Verses 7 and 10 cite a ransom for life. The world did not have one, but Israel did through their animal sacrifices, which pointed to the Lamb of God who would die for the sins of others.

The high point of this psalm is its affirmation of faith: "Why should I fear in times of trouble?" (5).

The Bible has over 365 commands to fear not, a different one for every day of the year. David, Israel's shepherd king, wrote, "The LORD is my shepherd … . Even though I walk through the valley of the shadow of death, I will fear no evil, for you are with me … . Surely goodness and mercy shall follow me all the days of my life, and I shall dwell in the house of the LORD forever" (Psalm 23:1, 4, 6).

Psalm 87

A Psalm of the Sons of Korah. A Song.

¹*On the holy mount stands the city he founded;*
²*the L*ORD *loves the gates of Zion*
more than all the dwelling places of Jacob.
³*Glorious things of you are spoken,*
O city of God. — Selah

⁴*Among those who know me I mention Rahab and Babylon;*
behold, Philistia and Tyre, with Cush —
"This one was born there," they say.
⁵*And of Zion it shall be said,*
"This one and that one were born in her";
for the Most High himself will establish her.
⁶*The L*ORD *records as he registers the peoples,*
"This one was born there." — Selah

⁷*Singers and dancers alike say,*
"All my springs are in you."

This chronologically last psalm written by the sons of Korah is their most important one for Gentiles. Its first three verses are an obvious tie to Jerusalem. Its last four verses are symbolic, unpacking a veiled contrast in verse 2. "All the dwelling places of Jacob" means Old Covenant Jews wherever they lived in Israel and beyond. As dear as

213

God holds their habitations, His greater love is the gates of the "city of God," where Gentiles can enter into the New Covenant.

The mention of Rahab in verse 4 gets readers off track. We think of the harlot heroine of Israel's conquest of Jericho (Joshua 2:1–21; 6:22–25), who ends up in Jesus' genealogy (Matthew 1:5), in Hebrews' hall of faith (Hebrews 11:30–31), and James 2:25. But the Sons of Korah used a different word here. Her name is the Hebrew *rachab* (silent c), meaning "breadth." Their word here is *rahab*, meaning "tumult." It is used as a poetic and symbolic name for Egypt, here, as the NIV footnote explains and in Psalm 89:10 and Isaiah 51:9. Switch Rahab to Egypt, and verse 5 names five places where Gentile people were hostile to Israel at some point. Five is the Bible's symbolic number for grace, which is how non-Jews become covenant believers by God's amazing grace.

The real key to unlocking this psalm is the word "born" in verses 6–8. The sons of Korah may not have realized it, but when the Holy Spirit inspired them to use this word three times here, His deeper meaning was "born again."

Centuries later in Jerusalem, Jesus would explain this to Nicodemus, a ruler of the Jews and teacher of Israel (John 3:1–10). Jesus told this Old Covenant religious leader, "Unless one is born again he cannot see the kingdom of God" (3:3) and "unless one is born of water and the Spirit, he cannot enter the kingdom of God" (3:5). He also said, "Do not marvel that I said to you, 'You must be born again'"(3:7).

Christ's threefold use here echoes the sons of Korah's verses 4–6 above. Their nice touch is verse 6, the Lord's record as He registers these births of "the peoples" (Bible phrase for Gentile nations). This is an Old Testament prophecy of the Lamb's book of life (Revelation 13:8, 21:27). Nicodemus could not understand Jesus' words that night in Zion, but he continued to ponder them. He was reconsidering Jesus in John 7:45. It was probably being in on Jesus' religious trial that changed his mind.

When Jesus was taken off the cross, Nicodemus helped carry him to the tomb of Joseph of Arimathea, bringing seventy-five pounds of spices to anoint the body (John 19:38–42).

The singers and dancers in Psalm 87:7 are celebrating salvation. In the parables of the lost sheep and the lost coin, Jesus speaks twice of joy in heaven and before the angels of God "over one sinner who repents" (Luke 15:7, 10). Let's join this heavenly joy when we learn of people being born again, especially when we have prayed for them, witnessed to them, or financially supported missions that helped reach them.

If the above interpretation of Psalm 87 bears witness with your spirit and you want to know more, or you're not sure about it but open to hearing more, the best elaboration I found is "The City of God" by Jim Shaddix, preached on September 18, 2018. His introduction is great but long, so forward it to 5:42 for thirty-three minutes well worth your time.

Shalom! Selah.

Acknowledgments

I thank the Lord for saving my dad in the year I was born. This changed and redeemed my life's trajectory. I thank God for Christian parents who raised me in the nurture and admonition of the Lord and brought me up in the church. I thank the Lord for all the church workers and leaders who modeled for me the Christian life and taught me to love God and His Word.

I thank the Lord for saving me at age eight and sparing me from much of the temptation and trouble that invades the lives of so many teenage boys and young men. I thank the Lord for instilling in me the confidence of how I am loved and who I am in Christ. "I can do all things through him (Christ) who strengthens me" (Philippians 4:13).

I thank the Lord for the family He gave me, starting with my wife Nancy and extending through fifty-four-plus years of happy marriage. I especially thank her for teaching in tough inner-city New Orleans schools to put me through seminary. As a girl, she told her parents, "I could never marry a Baptist preacher because they move so much." So I thank her for the eight geographic moves she was willing to make as I followed the Lord's call. She was a great pastor's wife in those congregations. We praise God that our sons, daughters-in-law, grand-daughter-in-law and ten grandchildren all know Jesus. We rejoice that seventeen of our family of eighteen are active in their churches.

"I thank him who has given me strength, Christ Jesus our Lord, because he judged me faithful, appointing me to his service" (1 Timothy 1:12). I thank God for the health and strength He gave me to pastor for a half-century. I thank Him for the good churches and the great association He allowed me to lead and for the pastor friends He gave me in each location.

I thank our heavenly Father for the Sons of Korah, the insights He gave me about their lives, and the call to put their story into print. I thank God for Lee McDerment, a twenty-first century son of Korah, who fanned its flames for me and helped keep this dream alive until the right time to finish the book.

Nancy and I praise God for our church friend, Beth Cuttino, whose life is an inspirational example of bouncing back after the bottom falls out on you. We sincerely appreciate her love gift to our Father in editing this book's first draft to make it so much better. In God's providence, she happened to be in an interdenominational Bible study on the Book of Numbers. Beth made this story more succinct, greatly enhanced its linguistics, improved the order of the chapter contents, suggested the helps resources, and even assisted with the research.

I thank Todd Deaton and Denise Huffman at Courier Publishing for turning my manuscript into a book. And I thank you for reading all the pages it took to get to this one.

Finally, since the sons of Korah wrote psalms and songs, I thank the Lord for my heritage in the hymns of our faith. I grew up on the Broadman Hymnal, then sang from iterations of the Baptist Hymnal. I can still sing from memory at least three verses in hundreds of hymns. Rarely do I hear a sermon or Bible study without a hymn line popping into my mind. There was nothing in my theology textbooks or the professor's lectures that the hymns had not already taught me.

Praise choruses have their place, and they energize worship, but I wonder how people in today's churches will learn theology. Hymns pop up in both passages on being filled with the Spirit. "Be filled with the Spirit, addressing one another in psalms and hymns and spiritual songs, singing and making melody to the Lord with your heart" (Ephesians 5:18–19). "Let the word of Christ dwell in you richly, teaching and admonishing one another in all wisdom, singing songs and hymns and spiritual songs, with thanksgiving in your hearts to God" (Colossians 3:16).

In God's timing, on the home stretch of this manuscript, I was back in the choir for the first time since 1974. My forty-nine years between choirs was one of the few real sacrifices I made to be a pastor. It doesn't work to be in the choir if you're the pastor or if you are attending 101 churches a year as their associational Director of Missions. (Good thing I've always loved going to church.) A month after we rejoined our current church, the music minister enlisted us as the choir began practicing its Easter musical. We were singing a short, sweet cantata I had never heard, then ending it with the Hallelujah Chorus. I learned its tenor part in high school. Our youth and adult choirs from First Baptist would go out to the new campus of First Methodist to sing it with their choir. This spring the Hallelujah had a double meaning for me. He keeps me singing.

Jim Goodroe
Jgoodroe2@gmail.com

THE ROMANS ROAD

"What is The Romans Road to Salvation?" asks Emily Hale at Christianity.com. Here's her answer:

God's plan for humans is communicated through the entirety of scripture. The Romans Road to salvation is a collection of verses from the New Testament book of Romans that concisely explains God's salvation plan. Because this collection is human assembled, not an official biblical arrangement, some collections may include more or fewer verses than others.

(All verses shown below are from Romans, the sixth book in the New Testament.)

Please read aloud the statements italicized below. When you can affirm the statements in one section, do this again in the next section.

The Human Problem
- *"As it is written: 'None is righteous, no, not one'"* (3:10).
- *"For all have sinned and fall short of the glory of God"* (3:23).
- *"For the wages of sin is death"* (6:23).

Humanity's Hope in Christ
- *"But the free gift of God is eternal life in Christ Jesus our Lord"* (6:23).

- *"But God shows his love for us in that while we were still sinners, Christ died for us (5:8).*

The Sinner's Response

- *"If you confess with your mouth that Jesus is Lord and believe in your heart that God raised him from the dead, you will be saved"* (10:9).
- *"For with the heart one believes and is justified, and with the mouth one confesses and is saved"* (10:10).
- *"For everyone who calls on the name of the Lord will be saved"* (10:13).

The Results of Salvation: Peace and Justification

- *"Therefore, since we have been justified by faith, we have peace with God through our Lord Jesus Christ. Through him we have also obtained access by faith into this grace in which we stand, and we rejoice in hope of the glory of God"* (5:1–2).
- *"There is therefore now no condemnation for those who are in Christ Jesus"* (8:1).

A Romans Road Prayer

(Silently read the prayer below. If you mean it, pray it aloud to God.)

God, I know that I am a sinner and that the wages of sin are death. I believe You sent Your Son, Jesus Christ, as payment for my punishment. I profess my faith for salvation through the death and resurrection of Jesus. I declare that Jesus is my Lord. Thank You for Your grace, peace, forgiveness, and eternal life. Amen.

(If you prayed this prayer and meant it, who should you tell that you have done this?)

The Jewish
Historical Writings

American evangelicals can be shocked the first time they see Bibles with different contents than ours. Some groups we would consider cults have their own distorted versions, which we dismiss out of hand. But others have our Old and New Testaments plus a section of fourteen books in between called the Apocrypha — from an ancient Greek word, *apocryphal*, meaning "hidden."

These books were written between 400 BC (the latest of our thirty-nine Old Testament books) and AD 200 (a century after the book of Revelation and as consensus on the New Testament canon began to emerge). These books are not considered "inspired by God," but there are histories in some of them, such as First and Second Maccabees. This is how we can view the Jewish writings of earlier periods. Though not divinely inspired, they can add historical details. Where not contradicted by Scripture or logic, they may help flesh out details in our Bible stories.

These Jewish writings fall into several categories. An overview I find helpful is from a tour guide I had in Israel, a very religious Orthodox Jew. I bought the first two volumes of "Discover the Land of Israel: A Guided Tour in Biblical Israel with Talmud and Midrash," by Yossi Maimon. Korah was not in these first two volumes, but these sixty-five short stories and the details Yossi added were interesting. Some of these sounded like workable scenarios, though without the authenticity of the canonical books in the Old and New testaments.

Yossi's explanation of the Jewish writings helped me better understand some references my book quotes or cites that I found in my other research on Korah. Christ-followers may know that the Torah is the law and is what Jews call the Pentateuch (what scholars call our Bible's first five books). But what are Tanach, Talmud, and Midrash? Here are my excerpts from "biblical sources," Yossi's two intro pages in his first two volumes:

God's Torah is composed of both the Written Torah and the Oral Torah, which explains in detail the Written Torah. The Torah, together with other Jewish writings of the Bible, is known in Hebrew as Tanach. Such Jewish writings are separated between the historical descriptions of Jewish life … . Up to AD 70, the Oral Torah never existed in written format. It was taught by memory from teacher to student, from father to son. After the fall of Second Temple and the destruction of Jewish life in the land of Israel, there was a fear that the surviving Jews would not be able to maintain the study of the Oral Torah and pass this learning on to future generations … . Rabbi Yehuda HaNasi, the leader of the generation, gathered all the Rabbis together and compiled all of their Jewish knowledge into two sets of writings. One set is the six books of Mishna, which deal with daily Jewish laws. The other set is called Midrashim, which includes all of their Jewish knowledge and wisdom known at that time. The meaning of the word "Mishna" comes from reciting over and over again the knowledge the student has, to carve it into his memory forever … . The Mishna … was written at a very high level … . There was a need to simplify … . This was done through discussions and debates of the Rabbis and became known as the Talmud. In the Mishna, Midrashim and Talmud, we find many parallel stories to the events that happened ... during the time of the Tanach. These stories give a special perspective to the stories described in the Tanach.

WHY STUDY THE
OLD TESTAMENT?

I grew up on the New Testament with the famous Bible stories from the Old thrown in for good measure. After all, we are New Covenant believers, and covenant means "testament."

The needle moved for me in 1971. The Sunday after we brought our firstborn home from the hospital, I walked down the aisle to publicly answer the call to ministry. Nancy sat on the back pew with six-day-old Rob in her lap. Seminary did not start for three or four months, but my application required the official vote of our church. Nancy had to apply for a job teaching school in New Orleans to support us three, since we were leaving two good jobs.

The Spirit impressed me that before I started paying to have people tell me what the Bible says, I should see for myself. So, I read it cover to cover before we moved. I devoured it, was never bored, and learned a whole lot. But not the kind of stuff they teach at seminary. They had an exam you could take to exempt Old Testament survey for students who had taken the course in college. I thought it would be a snap for someone with a semi-photographic memory, who had recently read the whole Bible, but it snapped me. I had never heard the terms used in most of its questions. So, my first course at seminary was Survey of the Old Testament, Part One.

For the rest of 1971, I took Old Testament survey. The rest of 1971 and most of 1972, I learned Hebrew. The Hebrew Bible reads from back to front, and the pages and words read from right to left. Its letters look as if they are from outer space, and they are consonants only. The vowels are tiny marks, look like chicken scratch, and can go on any of the four sides of a consonant. Seminary was not where I learned to love the Old Testament.

The Bible character I have most identified with is Moses. Like him, I had worldly success before spiritual impact. I was too serious for my high school peers, but this played well in my four years at our state's flagship university, followed by two years working with Southern Bell.

When the Levites were organized, and still in Jesus' day, public ministry began at age thirty. I started church work at age twenty-five but had little ministry impact until age thirty. God used two Old Testament stories to convict me that I was trying to minister in my own strength and for my glory. I'd read or heard them before, but it was just head knowledge.

When the small church I had pastored in seminary liquidated its library, I salvaged a small paperback, *The Saving Life of Christ*, by Ian Thomas. I'd never opened it. But one day, in a rare bout of despair at age thirty, my eye caught it on my bookshelf. The Spirit drew me to it and kept away all interruptions while I devoured it. Despite the title, most of its chapters were from the Old Testament. The Holy Spirit used two of them to pierce my heart and break my flesh. The first was about the burning bush and entitled "Any Old Bush Will Do." Moses thought it was the bush that was special, but any old bush will do — *if* God is in it. I had tried to become the best bush I could be for God, but I had to die to self.

Thomas' other zinger chapter for me was from 1 Samuel 15. Amalek was Israel's archenemy, so the Lord gave King Saul's army the victory. God had devoted Amalek to destruction and commanded the total extermination of them and all their possessions. "But Saul … spared

[King] Agag and the best of the sheep ... and all that was good, and would not utterly destroy them. All that was despised and worthless they devoted to destruction" (1 Samuel 15:9).

Within months of sitting under Jerry Vines' preaching, I had given up the shady side of the flesh. But six years later as a seminary graduate, ordained minister, and full-time Christian servant, I was still trying to do life and ministry in the self-righteous side of the flesh, being "the best bush I could be," for the Lord.

God's remedy was for me to confess and provide or offer restitution to two authorities I had cheated in my college years and to withdraw from my seminary's doctoral program in which I had completed all the on-campus work. I was doing the doctorate for the wrong reasons: my pride, and to open doors to bigger and better ministry positions.

I was amazed at what happened immediately. God gave me a deeper insight into Scripture, such as how the Old Testament applies to New Covenant believers. I began to experience a power in ministering His Word to the lives of people. In the days of cassette tapes, I cringed when I listened to sermons I had preached in my seminary pastorate. I threw them away, feeling sorry for what my listeners endured. In God's mercy to my next two congregations, I was a staff minister the next five years, preaching only occasionally.

The early believers who experienced the New Testament events had the Old Testament as their Bible and their background. The testaments complement each other. You may have heard, "The New is in the Old concealed; the Old is in the New revealed." A dynamic you may not have detected is that in general, the New Testament clearly spells out spiritual principles but rarely illustrates them in the lives of individuals, especially after the gospels and Acts.

The Old Testament reverses this. It fleshes out spiritual truths in and through the lives of individuals without expositing the truths themselves. One of the best illustrations of a Spirit-filled believer is Daniel. He lived in the Old Testament before the Holy Spirit indwelled people but only occasionally came upon a rare individual. The life Daniel lived seemed so supernatural that his pagan peers concluded that in him was the spirit of the holy gods (Daniel 4:8–9, 18; 5:11, 14). In this Korah story you read, I season the Old Testament prose with some New Testament principles.

The New Testament says, "All Scripture is breathed out by God and profitable for teaching, for reproof, for correction, and for training in righteousness, that the man of God may be complete, equipped for every good work" (2 Timothy 3:16–17). We want to profit from all sixty-six books of God's Word, not just its last twenty-seven.

Don't shortchange yourself of any profit by camping out in just the New Testament. Be complete, equipped for every good work the Lord may have planned for you. *Selah.*

How the Levites Were Special

"Then you shall say to Pharaoh, 'Thus says the LORD, Israel is my firstborn son, and I say to you, "Let my son go that he may serve me." If you refuse to let him go, behold, I will kill your firstborn son'" (Exodus 4:22–23).

The LORD said to Moses, "Consecrate to me all the firstborn. Whatever is the first to open the womb among the people of Israel, both man and beast, is mine" (Exodus 13:1–2).

And the LORD spoke to Moses, saying, "Take the Levites instead of all the firstborn among the people of Israel … . The Levites shall be mine: I am the LORD" (Numbers 3:44–45).

God promised to make a great nation of Abraham. But he and his wife Sarah had just one child, Isaac. Isaac had two children, twins Esau and Jacob. God elected the younger, Jacob, through whom to fulfill the promise to make a great nation from Abraham.

Jacob, whom God renamed Israel ("ruling with God," Genesis 32:28) had twelve sons and a daughter by two wives and their two maids, who were Jacob's concubines. You can imagine that a family with thirteen children by four mothers was dysfunctional, and this one was. In such a large family, children blend in, until they stand out by doing something really good or bad.

Levi and his brother Simeon stood out for something very bad:

deceiving and murdering all the helpless men in a Canaanite city, then plundering their wealth. Shechemites were trying to intermarry with the Israelites, starting with Levi's sister Dinah (Genesis 34). This enraged Jacob, who realized that repercussions would come, so he moved the family to Bethel (34:30–35:6). He never forgave this pair. On his deathbed when he blessed his other sons, Jacob pronounced a curse on this pair:

> *"Simeon and Levi are brothers; weapons of violence are their swords. Let my soul come not into their council; O my glory, be not joined to their company. For in their anger they killed men, and in their willfulness they hamstrung oxen. Cursed be their anger, for it is fierce, and their wrath, for it is cruel! I will divide them in Jacob and scatter them in Israel" (Genesis 49:5–7).*

Two of Jacob's pronouncements here on Levi would play out centuries later. Psalm 76:10 says to God, "Surely the wrath of man shall praise you; the remnant of wrath you will put on like a belt." When Moses was on Mount Sinai with God getting the Ten Commandments carved in stone by the finger of God, the faithless Israelites pressured Aaron to make the golden calf. Their idolatry and immorality below triggered God's wrath above (Exodus 32).

God and Moses refer to this wrath. God tells Moses, "Now therefore let me alone, that my wrath may burn hot against them and I may consume them ..." (Exodus 32:10). "But Moses implored the LORD his God and said, "O LORD, why does your wrath burn hot against your people, whom you have brought out of the land of Egypt with great power and a mighty hand? (Exodus 32:11). Moses descends to the people below, as the agent of God's wrath, which they have brought on themselves.

Then Moses stood in the gate of the camp and said, "Who is on the LORD's side? Come to me." And all the sons of Levi gathered around him. And he said to them, "Thus says the LORD God of Israel, 'Put your sword on your side each of you, and go to and fro from gate to gate throughout the camp, and each of you kill his brother and his companion and his neighbor.'" And the sons of Levi did according to the word of Moses. And that day about three thousand men of the people fell. And Moses said, "Today you have been ordained for the service of the LORD, each one at the cost of his son and of his brother, so that he might bestow a blessing on you this day" (Exodus 32:26-29).

The last sentence above reveals that some Levites had participated in the idolatry and immorality, and they paid for it with their execution by fellow tribesmen. Though Jesus had no sin of his own, at the cross, God executed His wrath against the sins of the world at the cost of His Son.

- *"For God so loved the world, that he gave his only Son, that whoever believes in him should not perish but have eternal life" (John 3:16).*
- *"And again, when he brings the firstborn into the world, he says, 'Let all God's angels worship him'" (Hebrews 1:6).*
- *"Jesus Christ the faithful witness, the firstborn of the dead ... to him who loves us and has freed us from our sins by his blood" (Revelation 1:5).*

As John the Baptist said when he pointed the crowd to Jesus:

- *"Behold, the Lamb of God, who takes away the sin of the world!" (John 1:29).*

- *"For Christ, our Passover lamb, has been sacrificed" (1 Corinthians 5:7).*

Most believers understand that the animal sacrifices throughout the Old Testament are a picture and prophetic type of Christ's death. But few realize the significance God put on the firstborn, whether lambs or other animals or even Israelites. This plays into how the Levites became God's special tribe.

God claimed all the firstborn in Egypt. He claimed the Egyptian firstborn in death and the Hebrew firstborn in life. But God realized that to set apart the firstborn in every Israelite family from then on would be disruptive to society. So He decided to take one tribe from the nation instead of one child from each family: "And the LORD spoke to Moses, saying, 'Take the Levites instead of all the firstborn among the people of Israel ... . The Levites shall be mine: I am the LORD'" (Numbers 3:44–45).

The Bible's fourth book got its name from the two numberings of the people (1:1–46; 26:1–51). We would call them a census, which ESV does. Why the second census? Many had died since the first one. My chapters have addressed several such mass deaths. The total counts were similar: 603,550 (1:46) to 601,730 (26:51), but some tribes lost as many as 37,300 (Simeon), and Manasseh gained 20,500. Each of these numberings was actually a military muster, counting just males age 20 and over who were able to go to war. If such man typically had a wife and two children, there would have been over 2,400,000 total Israelites at this time. With the first census, the Lord exempted the Levites to operate the tabernacle when it is set up and to move it and its furnishings (Numbers 1:47–53).

One of the Bible's most interesting passages is Numbers 3:40–51, which the English Standard Version titles "Redemption of the Firstborn."

Remember God took the Levites instead of the firstborn from all the families. Conveniently, these two numbers were very close when they counted males from a month old and upward. There were 22,000 Levite males this age (3:39), and 22,273 such-aged male firstborn in all the other tribes (3:43). Had you or I been in charge at this point, we would have probably said, "That's close enough. Let's call it a deal." But with God, every individual matters. Since God had claimed every firstborn male, the rest of the Israelites still owed Him for 273 firstborn. So God set a redemption price of five shekels for each of these 273 (3:46–51).

The golden calf incident prompted Moses to give the Levites God's call to "put your sword on your side"(Exodus 32:26). Thank goodness that the sword for New Testament Levites is the Word of God.

- *"Take... the sword of the Spirit, which is the word of God" (Ephesians 6:17).*
- *"For the word of God is living and active, sharper than any two-edged sword, piercing to the division of soul and of spirit, of joints and of marrow, and discerning the thoughts and intentions of the heart" (Hebrews 4:12).*

The sense in which we should act as an agent of God's wrath is in warning those who refuse to believe in Jesus to receive the gift of salvation God offers through him. "Whoever believes in the Son has eternal life; whoever does not obey the Son shall not see life, but the wrath of God remains on him" (John 3:36).

The second numbering was done for assigning territory in Canaan (Numbers 26:51–56). Jacob's prophecy that God would divide the Levites in Jacob and scatter them in Israel had an interesting literal fulfillment. Levi was not granted a specific territory for an inheritance as were the other tribes. Instead, they received by lot and lived in about four cities of each of the other tribes (Numbers 35:1–8; Joshua 21). This enabled them to instruct the people throughout the land in the law and in the worship of God.

Since priests were a part of the tribe of Levi, thirteen of these four dozen cities went to them and were located in the tribal area of Judah, Simeon, and Benjamin. The rest of the Kohathites received ten cities from the tribes of Dan and the western half-tribe of Manasseh. Gershonites got thirteen cities from Issachar, Asher, Naphtali, and the eastern half-tribe of Manasseh. Merarites got twelve cities from Reuben, Gad, and Zebulon (Joshua 21:1–8).

> The Levites were not the sole possessors or occupiers of these cities. They were simply allowed to live in them and have fields for the pasture of their herds. These cities did not cease to belong to the tribes within which they were located. The Levites … appear to have been regarded in some respects to the tribe within which they resided …. They are never regarded as a thirteenth tribe ("Levitical Cities," *Encyclopedia of the Bible)*.

Although the Levites did not own land in Israel, they possessed a special relationship with God.

> *Therefore Levi has no portion or inheritance with his brothers. The LORD is his inheritance, as the LORD your God said to him (Deuteronomy 10:9; 18:2).*

> *For the LORD your God has chosen him out of all your tribes to stand and minister in the name of the LORD, him and his sons for all time (Deuteronomy 18:5).*

A modern illustration of this is the pastorium (parsonage/manse/ rectory/vicarage), a house owned by the church, where clergyman live. Since the church maintains it, its occupant is free from dealing with maintenance concerns. Such arrangements were very common until the last third of the twentieth century, but concerns by both parties have made them the exception today. My family spent a dozen years in two pastoriums, then bought the house from the pastorate to which we moved.

My impression has been that most clergy have enjoyed being the modern manifestations of the tribe of Levi. Every career has its negative aspects, but ministers get to spend much of our work week studying and teaching the Bible, ministering to people, and pointing people to the Lord.

Printed in the USA
CPSIA information can be obtained
at www.ICGtesting.com
LVHW021744131023
761031LV00037B/764